Recording Techniques
of the Guitar Masters

Brian Tarquin

Course Technology PTR
A part of Cengage Learning

COURSE TECHNOLOGY
CENGAGE Learning

Australia • Brazil • Japan • Korea • Mexico • Singapore • Spain • United Kingdom • United States

COURSE TECHNOLOGY
CENGAGE Learning®

Recording Techniques of the Guitar Masters
Brian Tarquin

Publisher and General Manager, Course Technology PTR: Stacy L. Hiquet

Associate Director of Marketing: Sarah Panella

Manager of Editorial Services: Heather Talbot

Marketing Manager: Mark Hughes

Acquisitions Editor: Orren Merton

Development Editor: Cathleen D. Small

Project Editor: Cathleen D. Small

Technical Reviewer: Lorenz Rychner

Copy Editors: Laura R. Gabler and Donna Poehner

Interior Layout Tech: MPS Limited, a Macmillan Company

Cover Designer: Luke Fletcher

Indexer: Sharon Shock

Proofreader: Megan Belanger

All trademarks are the property of their respective owners.

All images © Cengage Learning unless otherwise noted.

Library of Congress Control Number: 2011936037

ISBN-13: 978-1-4354-6016-4

ISBN-10: 1-4354-6016-2

Course Technology, a part of Cengage Learning
20 Channel Center Street
Boston, MA 02210
USA

Cengage Learning is a leading provider of customized learning solutions with office locations around the globe, including Singapore, the United Kingdom, Australia, Mexico, Brazil, and Japan. Locate your local office at: **international.cengage.com/region**

Cengage Learning products are represented in Canada by Nelson Education, Ltd.

For your lifelong learning solutions, visit **courseptr.com**

Visit our corporate website at **cengage.com**

Printed in the United States of America
1 2 3 4 5 6 7 13 12 11

*To my beautiful, understanding wife Melissa, who has encouraged
me to take up the pen and write down my music knowledge,
and to our awesome children, Liam Tarquin, Brianna, Bette,
and my devoted mom, Pema.*

Foreword

When you become obsessed with the guitar, you're also seduced into an eternal quest for tone. It's a one-two punch that no truly serious guitarist can avoid. As soon as your fingers can negotiate the basics of chord forms and single-note melodies, you're off into the never-ending search for better sounds, cooler effects pedals, transcendent amplifiers, clearer pickups, more articulate or warmer strings, and so on, and so on, and so on.

And then there's the recording studio—a sacred sonic sanctuary where even more timbral options are arrayed before you. The kicker here is that, unlike live performances where explicit and specific tonal constructs can be lost to the mists of memory (unless, of course, the gig is recorded), studio recordings document your brilliant or terrible guitar sounds forever. In short, you don't want to mess up when a very sensitive and unforgiving microphone is pointed directly at your acoustic guitar or your amplifier. Like the highwaymen of yore, the guitarist must "stand and deliver" and unleash a thrilling performance and an ear-catching tone. Anything less is risking public dismissal, disinterest, or outright disrespect. Not a lot of room for error, huh?

Perhaps this is why—several decades forward from Les Paul's astounding home-studio productions—many guitarists still get a bit unhinged when that red light goes on and recording is happening *right now*. Even with all the advantages and shortcuts that modern technology has provided today's musicians—the excellent digital-amp models, the fabulous quality of affordable instruments, the dazzling number of signal-processing parameters, and truly accessible and high-quality recording equipment for musicians who want to record in their homes and rehearsal spaces—fear and indecision can flame out a tracking session as fast as a power outage. Panic such as this is nuts, unproductive, and unnecessary.

Admittedly, today's guitar player is faced with an abundance of paths to tonal glory or sonic suicide. Every part of the signal chain, from the guitarist's hands to the amp to the mics to the plug-ins employed in crafting a sound, have the power to kill beauty. But that's a pessimist's view of the recording process. All of these tools can also enhance your own unique sound to the point where people simply can't disengage their ears from the majesty of your recorded performance. Hey, it could happen!

The first step to manifesting success, rather than sad and totally lame failure, is simple. It's knowledge.

Now, while all the experience and book learnin' in the world can't guarantee talent and popularity—see, you're starting to surrender to pessimism again—they can absolutely help any player get closer to documenting his or her creative ideas. Knowing what you want and what tools and techniques you need to get there are critical elements in the recording of a bigger, more incredible and alluring you. Trust me on this: a spectacular guitar tone, a great part (whether that part is a riff, a lick, a solo, or a chord progression), and a fiery performance are the main components of all classic and legendary guitar recordings. We'll leave the performances and the parts to you. As for the tone—never fear. This book is here to give you the ammunition to deliver something wonderful.

The author, Brian Tarquin, knows his way around a recording studio, and he has the career successes and groovy awards to show for it. By himself, he could provide enough save-your-butt advice to get you churning out super-hot guitar sounds in your home studio (or in any studio, large or small, for that matter). But the genius of *Recording Techniques of the Guitar Masters* is that Brian is combining his own recording knowledge with the actual techniques used by guitar superstars to produce their most guitar-rific tracks. That's like having sorcerer power, man! How can you miss? Devour this book like a starving panther, and you'll soon find yourself crafting guitar tones that *rule*. If you study hard, inspiration and application will visit your brain so often that you'll risk becoming a studio hermit who only exits his or her creative space for fast-food runs and the occasional shower. (This approach is not recommended, by the way—seeking balance in life is always the smart, and healthier, move.)

As this book will likely solve all of your guitar-tone challenges in the recording studio, I'll leave you with three (hopefully) productive tips of my own.

Have No Fear. Remember, you are recording sounds that can be erased or ignored. None of your ugliness has to see the light of day. You can submerge it. Kill it. Destroy it. This is why I never get "red-light fever" or get nervous while recording even the most challenging guitar parts. I know that all of my suck-itude will exist for my ears only. The audience will only hear the good stuff that I choose to release to the public. So, why worry? You are in control. Remember that.

All Options Are Viable. Guitarists tend to agonize too much over some baffling and uncharted definition of what a "good" guitar tone is. However, real-world experience shows that all kinds of different guitar tones are present on classic and modern recordings. Big tones, thin tones, saturated tones, buzzy tones, crystalline tones, lo-fi tones, hi-fi tones—they all show up in recordings that actually sell to significant numbers of the music-buying public. So don't worry yourself to a frazzled nerve ending in an obsessive attempt to absolutely nail Jimmy Page's tone on "Whole Lotta Love." Just craft a guitar sound that feels right to *you*, and that supports the mood, vibe, and energy of the song you're giving it to.

Don't Do It "Right"—Just Do It. The talented, but crazy-ass '60s British music producer Joe Meek used to say, "If it sounds right, it *is* right." Great advice. What this means—at least to me—is that experimentation and the joy of doing can sometimes trump "expert" recording experience. You don't have to know the ins and outs of mic placement, acoustics, signal processing, or tube-amp circuitry. You can simply mess around with stuff until you produce something that knocks you out. How liberating is *that*? Now, stop worrying, and *start recording*!

Michael Molenda, editor-in-chief of *Guitar Player* magazine

November 2011

Acknowledgments

Props go out to the following artists and manufacturers who helped make this book a reality: Steve Jackson at Pulse Technologies, Mark Seaman at JDK/API, JoAnn and Tony at Industrial Amps, Mike Robinson at Eastwood Guitars, Mark Loughman at BAE, Jonathan Pines at Rupert Neve Designs and sE Microphones, Brandon Ficquette at Seymour Duncan, Malcolm Toft at Trident, Alex Perez at Fender Guitars, Brian Perera at Cleopatra Records, Billy Sheehan for his brilliant playing on "Blue Wind," Steve Morse for his great tone on "Towers," Frank Gambale for shredding it up on "Spanish Harlem," Chris Poland for playing his butt off on "Tarquinius Maximus," Gary Hoey for the great guitar playing on "El Becko," Randy Coven for those long nights of total bass debauchery, Hal Lindes for his enormous contribution on so many *Guitar Master* tracks, Chuck Loeb and his jazz shred on "Peg" and "Swift Kick," Andy Timmons for tearing it up on "Manhattan," Will Ray and his major mojo on "Constantinople," the Flyin' Ryan Brothers for double harmony shred on "Chopper Mania," Howard Hart, a true pro and kick-butt player on "Hell Kat," Alex De Rosso for his Italian guitar flare on "Stormy," and James Ryan, the lethal guitarist from Down Under who has contributed so much to *Guitar Masters*!

I'd like to specifically thank the following talented people for their contributions:

- Mike Molenda for his constant contribution to *Guitar Masters* and for his smooth and extremely well written words, not only in the Foreword, but also in his monthly dose of true guitar mojo in *Guitar Player* magazine. And anyone who can put up with my obsessive guitar fanaticism is a real trooper! You're the best!

- Geoff Gray: the man, the myth, the legend! I got my start at his studio in NY, Far & Away Studios, and I am still fascinated by all of his stories and knowledge! He is my label partner and is like a brother!

- Cathleen Small for her grooming of my manuscript. Truly, an editor's job is not easy, but it should be respected greatly. Thank you!

- Lorenz Rychner, editor-in-chief of *Recording* magazine, who enabled me to voice my guitar opinions in the magazine. Love those ELKS!

- John Heidt, for his liner note contributions to *Guitar Masters* and his loyalty to my guitar playing and style through the years at *Vintage Guitar* magazine.

About the Author

Brian Tarquin is a multi Emmy Award–winning guitarist/composer and has established himself as a top-rate TV composer/recording artist and owner of Jungle Room Studios. In 2002, 2003, and 2005, he won Emmys for Outstanding Achievement in Music Direction and Composition for a Drama Series, and he has been nominated for an Emmy seven times. Tarquin graced the Top 20 Billboard Charts back in 1997 with the commercial release *This Is Acid Jazz, Vol. 2* on Instinct Records, followed by three solo jazz albums, which generated several Top 10 radio hits on the R&R and Gavin Charts in Contemporary Jazz in the late '90s.

From 1996 to 2001, Brian recorded four solo albums—*Ghost Dance, Last Kiss Goodbye, Soft Touch,* and *High Life*—and has appeared in more than 12 Instinct compilations, selling more than 140,000 records in his career. In 2008, Tarquin produced and wrote *Fretworx*, which showcased new recordings by guitar greats Steve Morse, Billy Sheehan, Frank Gambale, Andy Timmons, Will Ray, and many others. The album features exclusively released tracks inspired by those who lost their lives on 9/11—a portion of the profits were donated to the Friends of Firefighters 9/11 foundation. It also contains rare tracks from Steve Vai, Santana, and Tommy Bolin, plus personal liner notes written by Hal Lindes of Dire Straits.

Some of Tarquin's accomplishments include writing the theme music for MTV's *Road Rules* and composing music for many other TV shows and films, such as *CSI*, ABC's *Making the Band, Extra, TMZ, Alias, Girl-friends, Ghost Whisperer, Good Morning America, Grey's Anatomy, Inside Edition, Jeopardy, 60 Minutes, The Bernie Mac Show, The Insider, The Nanny, The Parkers, The Simpsons, The Tyra Banks Show, Replicate, Chill Factor, The Sender, The First $20 Million Is Always the Hardest,* and *The Watcher*. In 1998, he formed the rock/electronica band Asphalt Jungle, which debuted with the CD *Electro Ave* receiving critical acclaim. *Electro Ave* incorporates funky big beats with metallic percussive guitar riffs and features the MTV *Road Rules* theme, "Witchcraft." It also contains the track "Tinsel Town," which was heard by millions of *Making the Band* viewers. With a unique style, Asphalt Jungle blends live raw guitar tones with fast-paced, bottomless grooves.

In 2006, Tarquin opened his own boutique record label called BHP Music, Ltd., specializing in instrumental guitar music. Starting in 2007, the label released the acclaimed guitar compilation series *Guitar Masters*, which features guitar legends Jeff Beck, Joe Satriani, Steve Vai, Les Paul, Zakk Wylde, Stanley Clarke, Billy Sheehan, Leslie West, Gary Hoey, Allan Holdsworth, Chris Poland, Chuck Loeb, and many others. The compilations, which were recorded, compiled, and produced by Tarquin at Jungle Room Studios, received rave reviews from the editors-in-chief of *Guitar Player* magazine and *Vintage Guitar* magazine, who both graciously contributed the liner notes for the compilation.

Contents

Chapter 4
In the Mix with Great Dynamics, Mic Pres, and Effects Processors   107

Chapter 5
Microphones for Tones   131

Appendix A
iTunes Best Guitar Songs   147

Appendix B
YouTube Best Guitar Videos   153

Companion Website Downloads

You may download the companion website files from www.courseptr.com/downloads. Please note that you will be redirected to the Cengage Learning site.

1 Guitar Recording Then and Now

One of the great things about recording music in general is that you are able to capture that moment in time, and little is more important than recording a great guitar solo or riff that is saved for all future generations to hear. Just imagine being able to document that great tone or genius performance so you can repeatedly hear it back. This is the fantastic thing about recording; it is a signature in time of your personal accomplishment in music. Just think of those landmark guitar recordings that we have today from deceased artists such as Jimi Hendrix, Stevie Ray Vaughan, John Entwistle, Tommy Bolin, Brian Jones ... the list goes on and on. But we would not have their music without the invention of recording, for which we can thank our great forefather, Lester William Polsfuss—better known as Les Paul.

Shel Talmy, 1960s Guitar

I wanted to start off the book with a real old-school producer, talking about how he recorded guitars back in the early days of the British invasion, and the person who comes to mind is Shel Talmy. He recorded the Who singles "Anyhow, Anyway, Anywhere," "I Can't Explain," "I Don't Mind," "I'm a Man," "Motoring," "My Generation," "Shout and Shimmy," and "The Kids Are Alright," plus the Kinks singles "You Really Got Me" and "All Day and All of the Night." Additionally, he produced other illustrious bands such as the Small Faces, Manfred Mann, and David Bowie's early days as Davy Jones. It was interesting to talk firsthand with a producer who worked on the edge of technology and learn how he achieved the sound of those early rock greats.

How did you get your start producing and engineering the Who?

I started out as a recording engineer here in Los Angeles. So a lot of what I did in England was use techniques I worked out here before I got there. When I got there, I realized that nobody was using those techniques. I was being told at the time that my sound was very different. In England during 1964, engineers were only recording with three or four mics on the drums and one on the guitar amp; it was pretty simplistic. They were not able to capture the drive and raunchiness that rock was supposed to have, or what I thought rock was supposed to have. The English techniques of recording were too polite, and I wasn't going to be polite. The Who came about...well, everybody knows that story. But I was working with the Kinks, and the Who's manager approached me to hear his band at an

1

old church where they were rehearsing. It only took about five bars for me to hear him say, "This is a great band," so I signed and we recorded "I Can't Explain."

How did you record the Who?

When recording them, the first thing I did is use about a dozen mics on Moonie [Keith Moon]. At the time, this was a very new technique that no one was doing in England. People said you couldn't use multi-mics because they would phase each other out. I just replied that we'd have to just wait and see. Ironically, about a month later everyone was using 12 mics to record drums. For guitar I used a lot of isolation to try to capture feedback. So on Townshend's guitar, I used three different mics—one long distance, one close, and one ambient—and combined them all, because we were only working with three tracks, of course, and what came out, came out. As far as mics I used on the guitar, it was so long I don't really remember, but it was probably Neumanns.

In 1964, when I recorded the Who, I was at IBC Recording Studios in England and used what they had as far as microphones. I never believed in recording tracks one instrument at a time—you lose everything to do with feel. In any event, everybody was doing it live, which was a totally different mindset in what would happen later. We were limited with tracks at the time and bouncing down tracks; losing a generation would make a difference. Dolby was just coming into existence, and I don't think anyone had them until another year later.

What type of recording consoles did you use at IBC?

Everybody built their own; there were no Neves around at the time. So IBC built their own [consoles]. Olympic built their own, and each studio would start out with something and add their own components. So there were no preconstructed consoles available at the time. IBC was certainly an innovator in terms of consoles. They had anywhere from 24 to 36 inputs in their consoles. Because there were only three track recorders, they felt that it was enough because premixing had to go on before recording. I spent a lot of time on baffling the instruments, because I thought isolation was one of the major problems that was going on in the industry. Actually, in LA I worked on different types of isolation and baffling, which was knowledge I brought to English studios.

Where we recorded the Who was an old Georgian building that had a preservation order on it. They had elaborate ceilings that I couldn't touch, so we had to put acoustical treatment around them. We put the drums in one corner, and I isolated them with screens, and then we would find a good spot for the amps. For acoustic guitars I used two U 87s, one pointing at the sound hole and the other at the fretboard, and then I would combine them. I also would use an 1176 with a little EQ, which would give more apparent level to the acoustic. I did this with the Pentangle record, which I was very pleased with the guitar sounds.

Did you both produce and engineer for the Kinks and the Who?

I mainly engineered the mixes in the beginning, and once I decided I was comfortable with it, I moved on to producing. I truly believe that you can't [both] engineer and produce accurately, because they are at either ends of the scale. Today it is a little easier, but you can't do an A1 job on both jobs at the same time. So I just moved strictly to producing.

The reason I used IBC and Olympic studios was because they were far ahead of everyone else for recording equipment, in the way they maintained and the way they continually looked to improve it. So the studios themselves, which in those days were all tube, built a lot of the limiters, compressors, and mic pres. The trick was then to record everything as good as you could get it, so the next step in mixing would go together very easily. Because with three tracks, once it's recorded, there is not a whole lot you could do, so I would be tweaking, combining, and EQing when I had to.

As far as editing was concerned, I started editing freehand before editing blocks came on the scene. I tried to keep editing at a minimum and track to get a perfect take. At the time, it was a singles market, so we just recorded tracks. The format at the time was ½-inch three-track, and we mixed it down to ¼-inch two-track. I would go three to three and then mix it down.

To get the job done, you were constantly bouncing. For example, I recorded "You Really Got Me" with the Kinks specifically because the head of Pye Records at the time, named Louie Benjamin, decided he was going to charge me for the studio time. So I recorded it in mono, because it was cheaper than multitrack. But when the single was a smash hit, things changed, and I wasn't going to be charged studio time if we did it in multitrack.

How did the sessions evolve?

I always believed the bands had to be well rehearsed about 90 percent, so I leave the 10 percent for spontaneity in the studio. We never did more than nine or ten takes. I used a lot of studio musicians, such as Jimmy Page, Bobby Graham, and Nicky Hopkins. I used them in adjunct to the band. For instance, the Who didn't have a keyboardist, so I brought [Nicky Hopkins] in to play, as well as with the Kinks. I brought Jimmy Page in on the first Kinks record as rhythm guitarist because Ray [Davies] didn't want to sing and play guitar at the same time. There is no question that Jimmy didn't play lead guitar on the album—that was all Dave [Davies]. Dave is a very underrated guitarist in his own right. I also brought in Jon Lord from Deep Purple in those sessions.

I brought in Bobby Graham for the Kinks sessions because they didn't have a drummer at the time. I always rehearsed everyone before we went into the studio, because I don't like surprises and I wasn't sure what the hell was going to come out the other end. I am a hands-on producer. I was always there from day one to the last day. I helped arrange and organize everything.

When Ray came in from the Kinks, he'd come in with a dozen songs, and we'd sit down at the piano, and I would say, "Yes, that's great" or "That needs more work" or "Let's put that one aside." The song "Sunny Afternoon" is a good example. He played me eight bars of it on the piano, and I said, "That's our next single." Also the song "Tired of Waiting": I pulled it off the LP and released it as a single, and it went to number one. I noticed that my records were always louder than others. I used to bring up two channels at the same time, one that was heavily limited—I'd keep it under the other track. This helped push up the apparent level, so in the final product it would always sound louder.

How do feel about the new digital age with so many options at your fingertips?

Oh, I love Pro Tools because it evolved into something extremely special. It's a pleasure recording with Pro Tools these days, because there are so many options and hundreds of ways to do things. You take bits and pieces of one track and combine with another. This was all a distant dream back then. When Pro Tools started there was a distinct difference, but there is no difference from analog today. There is virtually no difference (digital versus analog) except to an extreme expert, and I'm not even sure they could tell. When digital first came, they weren't capturing any of the atmosphere; it was all flat and bland. As digital started to progress, it started to capture all of the overtones.

I just finished mixing a CD for a band on Pro Tools, and it was an absolute pleasure doing it because you can't even tell it wasn't done analog. I did it at a studio where they have a lot of analog gear—1176s and LA-2As, stuff like that. It's a pleasure not to have to deal with the tape hiss. To be able to go back where you need to go in the track without having to wait for rollback on a tape machine is great. What I really hated was waiting while the tape was rolling back, to the point where we had to be—it drove me crazy. Today there is no waiting; you are there instantly. Very important for the band, so as not to lose momentum!

Barry Conley on Zakk Wylde, B.B. King, Stevie Ray Vaughan

The Fugitive Pope is a well-seasoned and top-notch engineer in Los Angeles. He recorded acts such as Stevie Ray Vaughan, Zakk Wylde, John Mayall, and the Red Hot Chili Peppers. Being a guitarist himself, he certainly knows his guitars and understands the whole process of getting a great guitar tone and utilizing the right microphones in recording. This is what makes him an exceptional engineer-producer. It was a privilege and pleasure speaking with Barry about his recording techniques.

How do you like to track guitar?

I started out working at a studio in Hollywood where I met my mentor, Robert Battaglia. Now he's got five Grammys for recording Bela Fleck. He used to work with Sly Stone and Wall of Voodoo, all these crazy bands. He was about five or six years older than me, so he had been in the business since the '70s. He kind of took me under his wing, and when I had a question I could go to him.

In the beginning, I was recording this LA punk band called Wasted Youth, and I just could not get the right guitar sound. The guitarist has a Marshall Plexi stack, which was unheard of in a punk band, but they were starting to go metal—this was around '85. I wanted to get a heavy sound, so I threw an 87 and 57 up there, and I just could not get that sound. So I ask my friend Bert what I should do, and he said to use a 57 on-axis to the speaker and use a 421 off-axis. The 57 is the bright and the 421 is the fatness, and of course there is going to be some phase cancellation, but it works for guitars. So I used that, and it worked great.

Another mic I use is the Sennheiser 409. It's a great microphone that also works great with a 57 but works even better with any kind of ribbon mic. The original 409 with the gold front and the ribbon mic [Beyerdynamic] M 160 work really well together. I worked with the guys from Queens of the Stone Age, and they use those mics a lot. I picked that up from those guys.

I like to keep both the ribbon and the 409 on the same axis to amp, so I don't get the phase cancellation; that way, both mics are the same distance from the diaphragm of the speaker. What I learned from Dave Royer himself was to keep the ribbon mics away from any blast of air, because that will tear the ribbon. Dave said never to put his mics in front of a kick drum, especially inside the hole. You really have to be careful. He said it's not the SPL; it's the blast of air energy that will rip it. Usually on a guitar you don't have to worry about that, so I get that thing pretty darn close, two to three inches away.

Once again I'm not a deep compressor guy, it just goes right to tape. Like with Zakk, all those records were done on analog tape. Whenever I hear records with compression, I think amateur. But for 10 to 15 years that's been the style; people use it for effect. But compression on a room mic can really liven up a drummer that is not that lively. When you listen to "When the Levee Breaks," Andy Johns is using Beyer 130s and compressing them through some Helios compressor going through one of those Echoplexes—it's just two mics and it's got it! The compressors are set so they are breathing with the tempo; it's amazing.

How did you record Zakk?

I kind of learned, doing that record with Zakk and Michael Beinhorn; Beinhorn would say those ribbons would react so fast because they have that small piece of corrugated metal. They react a lot faster than a dynamic mic, like a 57. You throw ribbon up there and you suddenly have something that is in your face. With Zakk I usually did the 57/421 combo, but when Beinhorn came into the mix, he used a Royer 121 ribbon. Suddenly the midrange thing was in your face.

Zakk really made me work and he is as loud as heck. This is what he does. He's got a Les Paul with EMGs, so you already got some really hot pickups. The EMGs have a lot of output, and back in the day Zakk would go through that Boss overdrive pedal—the yellow one; that was his secret weapon—and he'd have that thing cranked through the Marshall.

I think he used a JCM800; he loves them, usually the 50 watters, *cranked*! Then he goes into a Marshall cab that is loaded with the EV 200-watt speakers. Those things don't break up at all. So he's got the setup that is really overdriven hard to the cabinet and then the cabinet [is] brutal; it doesn't warm up the sound at all. It's not forgiving at all, but it works great in a stadium.

It is really hard in the studio. You can't tell him anything. He had a really bad experience with Roy Thomas Baker. Baker said the sound sucked, and he was just going to come in and mess with the sound. Zakk flipped. That was for an Ozzy record that he partially recorded, but he ended up getting fired from the project. Baker had these huge hits with the Cars and Queen and has an ego that goes along with it. The first thing he ever wanted to do with Zakk was to go touch his amp, too. Zakk said, "Don't touch my amp!" So for the first hour, he was freaking out and super uptight. So what I did was put a 57 and a 421 in a Neve 1073, and I loved it; that is one of my favorite preamps. And so I just tweaked the shit out of it. I had to boost the bottom end and then also boost the upper midrange to make it fat and bright, and I cranked the shit out of it. The Neve EQs are great, and it finally came together. That sound always works for me.

With Brian Setzer, I used the 57 and 421; he's already got that stuff set up on his rig live. I miked Zakk with a 414 only for acoustic guitar and on his Roland JC 120 for clean chorus stuff. I have a large amp collection, being a guitarist myself, and I always tried to get him to play the Supro, but he was locked into the JC 120.

With Zakk, if you reason with him, he'll come through. Zakk is an incredibly great guy. We had such a great time with the records I did with him, but I had to leave in the end because of some difficulties. I worked with a lot of rock stars, but man it was unbelievable what we could do and get away with because Zakk had a "get out jail" card wherever he went. He's a crazy guy. He went up to Les Paul once, kneeled down and kissed his hand, and Les said, "While you're down there, I got something else for you to kiss." And Les Paul doesn't know who Zakk is, and so Zakk said, "Yeah, Les, I got a guitar named after me," and so Les said, "I do, too!" Funny!

Zakk loves to tell stories, and he'll tell the same ones over and over again. He's really into Frank Marino & Mahogany Rush, so my brother once sent me a package and used an old Frank Marino record for packing, which of course got broken. So I brought it to the studio and put it up on the console for Zakk, and every time he started telling me a story he had told 10 times before, I would pick up that record and say, "Okay, Zakk, look at the record—you're sounding like a broken record!"

Who are some of the other guitarists you have recorded?

I recorded B.B. King at Paramount in the C room on a Focusrite console for an Arthur Adams record. Arthur Adams was really uptight that B.B. King was coming and they only booked a four-hour session. As always, I didn't have any help, so I had to set the whole thing up myself. So B.B. King flies in from Japan a half hour early, as I was plugging in the last microphone. B.B. sits down and says, "I want to play now," and I said, "I'm not quite ready—can you hang on?" and B.B. said, "No, I want to play now!" And then Arthur Adams says to do what he says! I had never worked on that board before, so I just threw the faders all up. It sounded amazing! I didn't have to do anything to it; that's how great the Focusrite was. And of course, all of my levels were fucked up, and there was distortion on the vocals. The funny thing is, we were done an hour early, and if they had given me a little more time I could've had this thing perfect. B.B. came in with a reissue Twin, and I miked it with a 57 and a 421 and put it in a couple of 1073s. It always seems to work for me. I stay away from 87s on guitar.

I recorded Stevie Ray Vaughan for a movie back in the '80s with Michael Keaton called *Gung Ho*. This was right after "Let's Dance" with David Bowie and his solo record, *Couldn't Stand the Weather*. The film company hired Stevie Ray to write half of the music, but the composer, Thomas Newman, kind of edged Stevie out. So they had Stevie come in and play over some of the tracks done by the composer. I was there from 8 a.m. until late night, after the film composer and engineer would leave. They didn't like hanging out with Stevie Ray; they were afraid of him. So Stevie and me would just hang out, and I would do mixes for Stevie for his archives. The respect wasn't there by the other people on the film for Stevie, but we just got along great. He always wanted mixes for everything, so at the end of the night I would make mixes of the different cues that we did on the film.

The last thing he said to me was, "Barry, never answer the phone when you are tired." I thought to myself, "What is he talking about?" About two years later, I was working over at Sunset Sound Factory, and they wanted to hire me on to become a staff guy there. I was taking a nap, and the studio manager called and said, "We really like you and want to hire you on and pay half of what you are making now." I said, "Sure, great, yeah, yeah." I hung up the phone and said, "I just agreed to work for half as much as I'm supposed to be paid! What was I thinking?" Oh Stevie Ray, never answer the phone when you are tired! Never make deals when you're drowsy. That has bitten me in the butt about four or five times. So I think what happened is Stevie Ray made a bad deal on that film. Like I said, he came with all this music and they were like, "No thanks!"

He did drop me some knowledge. So Robert Carradine showed up with a 1960 white Twin; I'd never seen one before. Stevie got some tools and loosened up all the screws on the amp and then tightened it all up again, super tight. He said, "This is how you play this amp," and he turned everything all the way up and said that you get everything from your fingers and the volume from the guitar. It sounded *incredible*!

We recorded him at Baby-O Studios, which had a Trident 80B console, in the B room. Of course, his main SRV guitar was completely beat up, filled with sweat—just dark wood with sweat bleached into it. He played like 15s on the highs and 60s on the lows. He also played an old Epiphone baritone guitar like it was a Strat with even thicker strings. There are only a couple of guys like Stevie that attack the guitar like that. Zakk is the other guy—full on. Because all the film people treated Stevie so bad, I was the only one he really took in, and Stevie at this time was on fire! His playing was incredible. It was a great time for music in LA.

What are your current projects?

A few years ago I got hired by the Art Institute in LA to teach. I really had to do some research; it's four hours a week I have to fill up, so I've been getting into recording techniques of other people. So I'm getting into the recordings of "Smoke on the Water" (Deep Purple), Frank Zappa, the Rolling Stones Mobile, great, great stuff. Right after I did Zakk's last record, things in Los Angeles really slowed down because everything changed. I was working at Paramount Studios for 18 years, which became a hip-hop studio, and

I'm a live guy. Since I did that last Zakk record in '07, everything there became rap and R&B, and I just don't want to do that. It's not necessarily that I don't like the music, I just don't like working with the people. Paramount was where all of the gangster rap was going on, and I've done those sessions and was happy to get out alive.

They used to have a Neve 8028; with all 1073 preamps in the C room that was killer! It was there for 10 years, and the rates were cheap. I did all sorts of great bands.

I'm building my own studio now. I bought some Trident A ranges from Cherokee Studios in Hollywood; I worked there for 10 years. I have a Pro Tools rig and some great outboard gear. I'm doing the no-console thing, mixing in the box.

Marc DeSisto, LA Guitars

Marc DeSisto is a successful Los Angeles engineer who started as a staff engineer in the mid-1980s with A&M Records, the old Charlie Chaplin Studio in Hollywood. During this time, he assisted on records for artists such as Pink Floyd (*A Momentary Lapse of Reason*) and Tom Petty (*Let Me Up*) and engineered on seminal records such as U2's *Rattle and Hum* and Don Henley's *The End of the Innocence*. Marc went on to be an independent engineer working with such artists as Stevie Nicks, Michelle Branch, Blondie, Jack Bruce, Robin Trower, and Buddy Guy and was nominated for a Grammy for his work on Melissa Etheridge's album *Breakdown*.

Tell me about the Robin Trower and Jack Bruce album *Seven Moons*.

I worked with Robin Trower earlier at a studio. He shows up with his Fender Strat and a couple of Fender Deluxes and said, "I know what to do with this!" So we did some guitar overdubs, a vocal and a rough mix. He really liked it. A year later, I spoke with his manager, and he said we were going to do a shoot out with different engineers for a new record with Jack Bruce. I said, "Of course, send it over." I sent over the mix, and they hired me to do the whole album.

How do you mike guitars?

My go-to microphones are a Shure 57 and a 414 together; I face them at a 45-degree angle with the two capsules touching, facing the opposite sides of the cones. I usually have a pad on the 414 and get a sound, and then I add the 57 slowly.

The trick is to get them both at the same level, so I have the guitarist give a G chord and I see where the peak is on the 57—say, –7 dB. I'd set the 57 to that –7 mark and bring the same thing up on the 414 and get that to –7. The way you see how accurate you really got it is you knock one side out of phase, adjust the mics so they are really canceling, and pop it in phase—and there's your sound.

Put the pan straight to 12 o'clock and blend the two mics together. The interesting thing is that the 414 gives the bottom and bright top tones, and the 57 gives the midrange tones, so this is where taste comes in. So when working as an engineer you set the tone—say one side is bright; then the other side you can make it a little darker tone by blending. So what you're doing is EQing with phase. That way you don't need to reach for EQ.

I rarely ever record guitars using EQ on them. Instead, I would move the mics to a different position to achieve various tonal qualities. When you blend both mics like this, the sound just jumps out of the speaker to you. You have to be patient because you have to listen to each mic, but when you put it all together, it's fat. I only put the one mic out of phase to make sure they are the same level; then I flip it back in phase, and they are really fat together.

Another combination for me is a 57 and Beyer M 160, which is an amazing microphone. They are the most underrated microphones ever. It's unbelievable. I did this track with Don Henley on *The End of the Innocence* album called "Heart of the Matter"—it's a Vox amp off of the floor and you hear it, it's so perfect. You know it can be magic if you put the right mic up. The 160 just has a beautiful, crazy midrange and top-end tone. Another combination is a 57 close and a U 67 maybe three feet away. I usually use this when I'm doing an overdub and want to fit in a different sound. If you listen to the old Queen records, you can hear some guitars that are close-miked, while others have an ambient sound. It might be a little hollower, but it works. Making them all work together and be harmonic is the trick. As an engineer, you're adding the colors and the tones by mic placement.

Mic pres and amps?

For guitars it is an API 312, Neve 1073 or 1081. API or Neve is what I would be looking for first. It's all about getting the ambience around the guitar correctly. I look around the room to see what kind of reflection is going to go back into the mic; if you are in a small room, you'll hear it. I may put the amp kitty-corner to get less reflection.

Certain amps, like a Vox, I try to keep off the ground, about a foot and a half, because I'm looking for the openness and the clarity of the 12-inch speakers. But the Bassmans I want on the ground, because they have only 10-inch speakers, and I want the floor to reinforce the bottom end.

My ambience mic is at speaker level and back about three feet. Generally I'm against rugs, but I may baffle the sides of the amp. This is all another way of working, so you don't need EQ. Sometimes I will mike a Vox from the back and put the mic out of phase because it has an open back, then place the mic off the cone's axis about an inch away. Get the sound off of the back of the speaker with a 421. That will be the same type of thing where you can blend the two mics together so you don't eat up two tracks.

For a closed-back cabinet, I will put it against the wall and bring some baffles in to concentrate on what's coming out of the cabinet. Also, I want to hear the cabinet with the guitar through and consider the song as well. It also helps to know beforehand, so I can get the mics set up. If I want that AC/DC fullness, I'll use a 414/57 combo, or if it is a jingly guitar part through a Vox, then I'll go with the 57/M160 combo.

With Mark Knopfler, I used the 414/57 to get his tone recordings. Actually, it was recording Mark's acoustic guitar that was hard. I wound up using a [Telefunken Ela M] 251, coming in at the 12th fret and angling it a few degrees towards the sound hole with a Fairchild on it.

Sometimes another thing I will do is put another mic over the shoulder—and it can be another little condenser room mic like a KM 18—and then blend it. I like to have a couple of different mics, so one is in phase and another is out of phase, so you don't have to rely on the one source. I do record guitars with effects. I will always record the effects on their own tracks. I have an old Time Machine box with a slap on it, phase, and other effects, that I will still use.

With U2, we printed the Edge's effects on separate tracks. Those guys were the hardest-working guys in the studio for takes and aggressive with getting the right sounds. They pushed each other in the studio. We miked the Edge with the 57/M 160 through a Vox and a couple of 87s in the room to capture a little left-to-right thing. It came out very bright and processed.

I like to always put two microphones on a cabinet, because the phase between the two speakers is never as good as just the one. I only use compression when printing guitars. Always go for a tube compressor—on guitar it can't be beat, especially the Fairchild. It's funny how every guitar player is so different with sound. Someone told me about Mick Ronson, that his amp was always set the same, but the variable was the wah pedal and where it was cocked in a certain position.

Analog versus digital?

In general, digital is a whole different parameter than analog. It's like using different paint. Remember when you were younger and Reese's Peanut Butter Cups were bigger, and now they are smaller? It's like, why are they smaller? Even though it's the same recipe, it tastes a little different.

I'm now getting used to the drum sounds with digital recording, but for guitar sounds I always prefer recording them on analog tape. Funny, as a kid when I was recording analog tape, I was fixated on getting the recording meters just right, not even really caring about the sound.

A mic pre is also a consideration; you may want a certain sound from overdriving a mic pre. The Clasp [Closed Loop Analog Signal Processor, by Endless Analog] is a new thing, and you need an analog console for it. You need a console to monitor it from, in/out, a tape machine, and Pro Tools. Basically, getting the sound from the analog machine and then recording into Pro Tools, coming off the playback head of the analog machine and then in digital. Digital seems to have the ceiling and a lack of depth.

When I was an engineer at A&M, I was an assistant engineer on Pink Floyd's *Momentary Lapse of Reason*, and they brought their own generator, 3M tape machines, an early version of Pro Tools, and Gilmour's amps, which were all 220 power. Our job was to overdub the drums, bass, and guitars on the demos they already did for the album. We did a shoot out between their 3M and our Studer machine; everyone liked the Studer—it had that depth, three-dimensional. So we took the 3M (because everything was recorded on the 3M) and bounced it down four tracks; then through SMPTE we locked the 4-track machine to the Studer 24-track machine and recorded all the new tracks on the 24-track locked to the master 4-track. We then edited on the 24-track and recorded back to the 3M with all sorts of edits. It was crazy! The SMPTE went dead at certain places with all the changes and edits. What a time, but it was so much fun and very exciting. But you can see why Pro Tools does have an advantage!

Andy Wright on Jeff Beck

Two of my recent favorite Jeff Beck releases are *You Had It Coming* and the 2003 album, *Jeff*. I love the way the fresh new break beat sound meshes with Jeff's awesome blues-rock licks, producing the driving, metallic sound of the turn of the 21st century. The man behind both productions is British producer-keyboardist Andy Wright, who really fused Jeff Beck into the 21st century.

I really loved the two releases you produced for Jeff Beck, *You Had It Coming* and *Jeff*. I thought they were very inspiring and progressive. Were there any particular artists or songs at the time that influenced you on the production?

Thanks; they are standout records for me in my 25-year career, particularly *You Had It Coming*. I was flattered to get the call from Jeff's management, and after meeting him I was inspired by his desire to create something fresh. I wasn't particularly interested in making records that only appealed to musicians, so I decided on something more beat driven. Artists that inspired me at the time were the Chemical Brothers, Fatboy Slim, and Leftfield.

Can you describe the creative process? Were the guitar parts written in the studio or already laid out or did Jeff come to the studio and just improvise?

We started with some basic ideas but not much in the way of concrete themes. I employed a beats programmer called Aiden Love, who was making beats that sounded like tracks in themselves. Both Jeff and I found them inspiring, so I set up 10-minute stretches of the most developed part of the beat, and we jammed to it. I played along with keyboards or bass lines, primarily to keep Jeff playing or perhaps to steer a change in mood. Over the course of up to 10 takes, Jeff would often do something that he would get off on and then follow it up with stretches of real inspiration that would often make up large parts of the resulting composition.

After this, I would fastidiously crawl through the performances that were recorded straight to Pro Tools. I had imaginary baskets that contained riffs, textures, rhythm parts, and interesting bits of soloing. First I would loop up textures or rhythm beds into two- or four-bar repeats onto individual tracks. I would then mute them and look through the riffs, choosing my favorite as the "chorus," and then loop that. After this, I would open up the textures or rhythm guitar loops underneath the riff until I found combinations that would go on to make up passages in the songs. Although this was time consuming and required a lot of focus, I found it thoroughly absorbing and, of course, I was working with amazing bits of playing.

What microphones were used to record the guitar parts? You can be as detailed as possible with miking techniques and preamps as well as processors. Take us through a little bit of the recording process and the gear.

Jeff's technician arrived for the preproduction with a Marshall JCM 800 top, a 4 × 12 cabinet, a Fender Stratocaster, and a Cry Baby wah pedal. We stuck the amp in the vocal booth of my programming room and stuck an SM 57 in front of the cabinet, about two inches from the middle. The mic was jammed at the other end into an Urei 1176, and from there, straight into a Digidesign 888. I had a Mackie (I think SR32) desk through which we monitored 24 channels from Pro Tools. It really wasn't much more complicated than that at any point.

Jeff created a huge variety of sounds with different combinations of settings both from the guitar and on the JCM 800. He regularly did takes with the Cry Baby set to a static position, which sounded really edgy, and I had a habit of cranking the Mackie desk EQs until it sounded like it does on the record. We often joked that Jeff would sound amazing playing a cheap supermarket guitar, and to be honest I would say that may be not too far from the truth!

I had booked two weeks' time in Metropolis Studio A, which housed a Focusrite desk. We were to record Jeff's band in there, and I anticipated a truck full of guitars, amps, pedals, et cetera, to arrive for this part of the project. When I turned up that morning, I saw Jeff's technician arriving in a car only to reposition the JCM, 4 × 12, and Strat in the vocal booth of Studio A. We recorded some valuable parts on those sessions, but by and large the guitars were recorded back down in my programming room. The lead guitars for "Nadia" and "Blackbird" were recorded in Studio A, and the sound was added to with the sound of the live room recorded on a Brauner VM1. The cabinet also had a Schoeps M 221 series mic directed at it. Jeff, however, seemed to prefer the intimate environment of the programming room. He positioned himself about a yard away from the glass door to the vocal booth and, as the soundproofing was not particularly good, he could partially hear the sound from the amp with the door closed.

How did you accomplish your vision of getting the guitar tone recorded? Was this discussed with Jeff beforehand or was it something that just came together in the studio?

It wasn't really a part of our conversation before we started working together, and, as it sounded great from the start, didn't really become a topic later. We were very much more concerned with what kind of music we wanted to make, the structure and form of the pieces. We were working at a phenomenal pace and did not get too sidetracked with technical issues. About five weeks into the process, Kaz (the A&R man from Epic records) flew over from LA and was totally blown away with what we were doing and insisted that we didn't change anything. This was just the impetus we needed, giving us the confidence to believe that what we were doing was special.

How do you go about getting the fat, beefy rhythm crunch sound on songs like "Earthquake" and "Loose Cannon"? It sounds as if there are several layers of guitar. What was the process?

This is covered largely earlier. I created the filter up section on "Earthquake" by utilizing the input on the Waldorf Pulse synth. I also had a selection of Lovetone pedals (the Meatball, Big Cheese, and Brown Sauce and also I think the Ringstinger ring modulator), which I fed some sounds through. The layering was very much a product of our system of editing loops of textures that Jeff played over the course of the day and combining them either with each other or the choice of riff. One thing that became very evident to me was how Jeff's technique created really unusual harmonics and resonances that were often almost impossible to replicate. Perhaps combinations of subtle vibrations and random cross resonances played a bigger part in this instance as we were looking for special parts that we repeated as opposed to long continuous performances.

Do you have a favorite can't-live-without guitar processor/effects that you used on the recordings?

On *You Had It Coming*, it would have to be the Cry Baby, and on *Jeff*, we used the Snarling Dog. The Lovetone pedals played an occasional part, but it was a very organic process.

On the beautiful song "Nadia," did you program the drum-n-bass groove beforehand and have Jeff play over it? Or were there multimusicians that came in after the basic guitar melody was laid down?

There was a different process for making this song, as it is a cover of the Nitin Sawhney track. I first worked out how Nitin had pieced together his version so that I could repeat the process with Jeff. Once I had the arrangement of melodies sketched out, I made a beat with Aiden and added the inspiring chords from the original with my Roland JD800 keyboard. There was a degree of construction, as we wanted to perfect the nuance of the singing on the guitar. Astonishingly, Jeff played the piece immaculately live, which is an incredible feat when all the quartertones and modulations are taken into account. With myself and Aiden in the programming room, we laid down pretty much all the rest of the arrangement. We carried this process through to the piece "Blackbird," which many people found inspiring, the bird song being even more complicated when you try and work it out in notation.

Anything you would like to add in terms of guitar recording tips or advice?

Get to know your instrument! That is the most inspiring thing about Jeff; he knows his instrument inside out as well as being a highly accomplished musician. Making something good is often more about music than technique. In this instance, it was also about challenging conventions. It is important to be original, and I find that most of the recordings I get from guitar students are just copies of other guitarists' playing style. While this is probably a good starting point in terms of technique, it won't get you noticed.

Flemming Rasmussen, *Ride the Lightning*

We all know how great those early Metallica records sounded, especially *Ride the Lightning*, *Master of Puppets*, and *...And Justice for All* for us guitar maniacs. The Danish engineer-producer behind the sound was Flemming Rasmussen and his Sweet Silence Studios, located in Copenhagen. These recordings of Metallica in the 1980s were revolutionary and had a strong influence for the time.

I really loved the three releases you produced and recorded for Metallica, *Ride the Light-ning, Master of Puppets*, and *...And Justice for All*. I thought they were very inspiring and progressive for that time period. Were there any particular artists or songs at the time that influenced you on the production?

I grew up with an older brother who started listening to the Rolling Stones when they released their first album in 1963. So my influence is almost any rock band from the mid-1960s and on, but at the time I did the Metallica albums, my favorites were amongst others: Deep Purple, Thin Lizzy, Led Zeppelin, Queen, et cetera. I had never heard trash metal before, but I love aggressive music with a "Tuff" sound.

How did the process go? Were the guitar parts written in the studio or already laid out? Or did the band come in the studio and just improvise?

Metallica, in that period, made very good demos, and all the songs were composed, arranged, and recorded on a very good demo. When we changed any of the songs, most changes were only slight.

What microphones were used to record the guitar parts? Take us through a little bit of the recording process and the gear.

All three albums were recorded analog on 24-track tape machines using Ampex 456 master tape. On the first two albums, all mics went through my Trident A-Range console. In those days we used the mic pres in the console. Very few people had external mic pres. On all of the albums the main mics are the Shure SM-7 and Neumann U 87, close-mics pointing to the center of one of the speaker cones. (Most guitars were recorded using two cabinets.) Then at an angle of 45 degrees from the corner of the cab and three to six feet away, I used AKG Gold-Tube mics, one on each cabinet. For room mics I used Brüel and Kjaer (now Danish Audio Design) 4006 omnis, approximately 10 to 15 feet away. On the first two albums, all EQs were the A-Range, and on *Justice* I used an old 1073-style Neve desk and had a B&B audio EQ inserted on the loop of the amp! That way, I could tweak the sound of the amp from the control room.

How did you accomplish Metallica's vision of getting the guitar tone recorded? Was this discussed beforehand or was it something that just came together in the studio?

On the first album, we tried to re-create the sound of one of James's guitar amps that had been stolen just prior to the session. But as for the final result on the albums, it was very much James and I who decided how it should sound, and we pretty much made it up as we went.

How did you go about getting that signature sound of the band's fat, beefy rhythm crunch guitars on songs like "For Whom the Bell Tolls" and "Battery"? It sounds as if there are several layers of guitar. What was your process?

All rhythm guitars are doubled at least once, and at places we have as many as six to eight guitars at the same time. James is just so tight that it sounds like one guitar. Some of the guitar sounds were made to fit or add to the main guitars, so when combined, it made that big sound we all liked.

Do you have a favorite can't-live-without guitar processor/effects that you used on the recordings?

Oh, yes. My old trusted Trident A-Range desk. And Urei 1176 LN and Shure SM7. As for guitar effects, I make it up as I go. I always listen to what the amp sounds like in the studio, and if I don't like it, I start tweaking. The source is always the most important. You can't save a bad guitar sound with EQs and compressors.

On the song "One," which became the band's big breakthrough song, how did you capture its many dynamics? Were the quieter parts recorded separately and then spliced together with the aggressive parts later? Or was it all laid down at once? Was instrument isolation an issue?

We recorded the different parts separately and made sounds for the specific part, and that included how we dubbed, et cetera, so every part sounded the best we could produce. All quiet parts were recorded separately, as were the clean guitars. And all guitars were dubbed in after we'd done the drum tracks.

Guy Charbonneau on Mobile Recording

During the past 35 years, Guy Charbonneau and his mobile recording studio Le Mobile have recorded and mixed productions for a wide range of talent within the music industry. His reputation for clean, pristine sound quality ensures a loyal following of clients. Guy recorded No Doubt's *Rock Steady* tour in Long Beach, California; *The Pretenders: Loose in L.A.* (DVD); and Kenny Chesney's *Back Where I Come from Party*. He also recorded and mixed tracks from the 2007 and 2010 *Crossroads Music Festival*, which featured more than 20 of the world's greatest guitar players. In addition, he recorded and mixed the live recordings of Gwen Stefani's *Harajuku Lovers Live* and her forthcoming *Sweet Escape Live* DVD.

He has also recorded such acts as Peter Gabriel, Rolling Stones, Stevie Ray Vaughan, Billy Joel, Genesis, Rush, Hall & Oates, Elton John, Santana, Squeeze, Foreigner, Lena Horne, Little River Band, Miles Davis, Bad Company, Prince, Grateful Dead—and the list goes on. Now those are some credits! But what really drew me to him was his audio recording of *It Might Get Loud* (a documentary on electric guitar) at the WB soundstage with none other than the godfather of guitar himself and my all-time favorite, Jimmy Page!

What are your approaches to recording live guitar?

Guitar sound onstage is very different from a controlled atmosphere of the studio, because you have the room, the PA, and the monitor. With guitar players, it has a lot to do with the guitar player himself, the amp, and the mic. A lot of new engineers feel they need a condenser mic, a dynamic mic, and a pod; it isn't better, just a different sound. I had a client once who had eight inputs from his guitar, preamps, effects, et cetera, and it's just not about that; it's about the playing. I always approach it so the guitar fits in the mix. Lots of times I use a Shure 57 or a Royer, but with a live show you are sort of tied to the venue.

Sometimes we have great sound because the sound becomes a part of the performance. I did *Crossroads*; we mixed 16 tracks of the show, and one of the famous guitarists loved the mix but wanted to have the Pro Tools session. So when he got it he cut up all of his guitar parts to be placed perfectly in line and remixed and sent it back to me. Well, all the feel was completely gone!

Sometimes I even mike the wedges onstage—it can be your best friend, being able to use in the final mix. I first listen and try not to be influenced where the mic is placed, but rather how it sounds.

What is the procedure for mobile recordings?

We have three systems to choose from when we go on the road for mobile recording: Le Mobile, the full truck recording system with the Neve 8058 (48 automated faders) recording console; Le Fly-Pak with 64 track of Pro Tools HD; and Le Box, a compact and affordable digital recording solution on the Nuendo system or on Pro Tools 9. Most of the time you tie in with the house PA lines; we have a 16-amp 220-line for power, or sometimes we have to rent a generator to give power to the truck.

I store the truck inside at our facility in San Diego and keep the air conditioning running all of the time. You always need circulation in the truck because it is insulated so well. Even when I was in Montreal during those cold winters, we had the air on to circulate the inside of the truck. Typically at night, when I store the truck, I keep the air at about 80 degrees and turn the equipment off. In places like Chicago, where the humidity is higher, you keep the air on all night, and then before turning on all of the equipment you put the air a little higher so no condensation happens.

The box of the truck size is 25 feet by 8 feet and weighs 52,000 pounds. I built the truck from the ground up with a special company that designs them and then took it home and installed the electrical system. Then I took it to a cabinetmaker to do all of the interior work, and we put in the insulation and traps as well. In 1980, I replaced the gas engine with the diesel motor and also repainted the truck.

What kind of reference monitors do you use in the truck?

My friend (who is an architect) and I installed the huge in-wall JBL studio monitors. We modified the position of the woofer—it has always been my main speaker for me. If it sounds great on the big JBL, it will sound great anywhere.

Through the years I've changed amps. I started with Crown, and now it's Bryston. Each speaker has its own amplifier, the tweeter, midrange, and eight-inch. I still use an old Urei Room EQ that is passive, and we modified it. Now 99 percent of the time near-field monitors are the way to go. I used to use Genelecs, KRK, and once in a while I'll have a guest engineer that will want to bring his own speakers. It is fine; the Tannoys sound great. Once in while you search for something new, and that's good. But don't listen on your computer—that's the worst thing.

How do you approach mixing in the truck?

The way I mix it, I try and do a full balance, a sort of vibe of the mix. We then bring in someone with fresh ears to listen, and then we tweak the solos and other parts. It's nice to have someone in with a new perspective. You leave your mix there, and the next day you come in. I'm the kind who'll put all the faders down; I don't care what I had yesterday.

When you start a mix, you try to push it, and sometimes you go too far, so you pull all of the faders back down. It's brilliant with Neve and the flying faders; it gives you a snapshot of the mix. You can compare yesterday's favorite mix and today's favorite. Hence when you start a mix, you have to find the direction and how you are going to push it. Sometimes you go back to your live monitor mix and say it's a lot better now. It may not be the perfect balance, but it has a better feel.

Sometimes I'll use the mic pres on the Neve, and sometimes the Grace; it all depends on the project. However, the bulk of the recording is the Neve. It's all digital recording today with Pro Tools—can't do a session without it. But there is something about the analog sound, the level and compression. It's very different from digital.

Another thing that makes a big difference to the sound is the input end of the preamp versus the output of the preamp. I always thought there was a difference. What I learned from Nick Blagona's recordings with Deep Purple is that with some preamps you're able to adjust the upward gain, adjusting the depth of opening and speech; you cut your input gain and the output and change the sound. But today's preamps don't have an upward gain; you just tend to look at the red in Pro Tools. This is not recording to me. It's like comparing old vinyl to CD—what a difference. How great those old records sound, not that CDs are bad. You are able to get almost 18 dB of audio on the CD, so each guy goes louder and louder. That's why mixes are in your face today, which changes the sound. In the analog days we weren't able to do that because you had to leave headroom for the mastering engineer. It's not the bit rate, it's the way you record it!

Favorite recordings?

Recording Rush was great; recording No Doubt and Gwen Stefani, loved it! They are super-nice people. I tried to capture what they do. Sometimes I hate myself, but I don't listen to my mixes. This year when I did Clapton, it was great. Jimmy Page, *It Might Get Loud*—that was cool, great! During recording, I put a Neumann M 149 on the table; it is a good-looking mic and worked well for the film. I remember the Edge came in the truck and said, "It sounds better in here than it does out there." These are the type of projects you enjoy, because you have a little more time to create something. It's the performance of the musician, not the machine.

Studio Tech Advice

One of the most important people in the analog studio chain is, of course, the unsung hero studio tech. This is one of the most important jobs, because, let's face it, when we're producing a record and the analog tape machine is out, or channels 5 and 12 are not passing signal, or our transformer is smoking in the guitar amp, we need to call a tech to get us back on track, no pun intended. My go-to guy here in the Hudson Valley is Chip Verspyck of Tech It Out Inc., a man worth his weight in gold for us diehard analog guys!

Give a little information on your background as a recording maintenance/amp tech.

I started out as a staff assistant recording engineer in New York City at Sound On Sound Studios and Chung King, and then switched over to being a maintenance/electrical engineer while at Bearsville Studios in upstate New York. It was a big facility, and there was always a lot to do keeping three—and at one point four—studios going that were all analog and mostly vintage. Pro Tools was in its infancy then, so everything got tracked to two-inch analog. It was at times some high pressure when those Studer machines would go down and had to be fixed in a super hurry with the clients waiting to get back to work.

People liked to work all hours of the night, and sometimes I'd get woken out of bed with a call to come in and fix a session stopper with the Neve or SSL console misbehaving, or a multitrack machine. I was an ER doctor for electronics on call 24-7.

As far as guitar and bass amps go, there was a modest but good house collection at Bearsville, but I'd often work on the amps belonging to the artists recording there. Guys like Derek Trucks would bring their own Fender with a blown rectifier over to me in the shop, or Paul Kolderie would rush over an Orange that smoked in a hurry because it went down in the middle of a take.

You should have seen Cheap Trick's guitar and amp collection! It filled an entire truck, and they had two guitar techs there with them, but no amp tech, so I was quite busy fixing a lot of amps! Most of the bands brought in a guitar and drum tech with them, but nobody knew what to do with their amps.

I left Bearsville full time 10 years ago and started working for myself under Tech It Out Inc. I do everything technical audio: electrical engineering, studio installs and design, refurbs and repairs, custom electronics design, acoustics and technical consulting. My workshop is in a high-end studio called the Clubhouse in Rhinebeck, New York. They have an incredible vintage guitar amp collection there.

Can you explain the essential difference between analog and digital recording and how it affects guitar?

I think the *essential* difference between analog tape and computer recording is the working environment. Tape limits your choices and makes you commit, forces you to work harder and perform better. If you can simply look at Pro Tools as just another tape machine and not an audio chopping block, you'll be better for it. Pro Tools just gives you too many choices and options; it can make you lazy or sloppy knowing you can do magic tricks on a crappy performance later. It can all get sterilized very quickly, a big vibe crusher. I'm afraid of it, and I don't have a clue how to use it. I stopped working as a recording engineer before Pro Tools was really on the scene. But really, set a properly aligned and biased analog tape machine side by side with a Pro Tools rig and record to both, and you tell me which one sounds better…to me there's no comparison. On the other hand, with the cost of maintenance and tape, less hassle factor, and speed of working, Pro Tools has the edge, no doubt.

A big problem I see is people picking up old analog machines for cheap and not seeing the hidden costs of maintaining them or not aligning them properly—or even at all, for that matter. I've seen a lot of machines totally out of whack and people using them thinking, "Oh, that's the sound of tape, cool!" And their high end is all messed up and distorted because the bias isn't right and the tracks are all phase shifted because the azimuth hasn't been adjusted in 10 years. Tape sounds very high fidelity, but it must be on a well-maintained machine that is properly aligned. When analog and big-budget facilities were the norm, staff techs would check and adjust the tape machines every morning.

For the guitarist, what are the must-have analog recording gear, compressor, mic pre, EQ, mixer, et cetera?

Your best-sounding recording gear is only going to sound as good as the performance and space you're capturing, so you should first put your dollars and efforts into making it so the acoustics of your room are good enough. You also need good, accurate monitors. A good recording engineer can make a rock-n-roll electric guitar sound good on most cheap recording gear as long as the amp, guitar, space, and player are good. People can make fantastic-sounding recordings with just 57s, a Mackie, and a four-track. For recording acoustic or clean electric, though, I'd invest in a few good-quality mics and a quality preamp.

Hi-pass filters are good for taking out the low-end rumble and junk that will fight with the bass and muddy it up. EQ is best left for mixing; it's better not to track with it. Get your tone set right at the source and use the EQ on the amp. Experiment with different combinations of amps and guitars or the placement of the mic before you grab for the EQ.

Can you explain to us the essence of compression and how it helps guitar, especially in hard-rock music?

Compression is making louder sounds quieter and softer sounds louder; it's the squeezing of sound volume. The more you compress, the less dynamic range you have. There's often not much dynamic range in hard-rock music, and that's because it often gets a lot of compression. Guitar amp distortion is an extreme form of compression. When your amp starts to distort, the crests of your sound waves are getting cut off as you run out of headroom, which limits volume; it only lets it get so loud. Add a tube rectifier, and you get even more compression as the power supply voltage sags down and limits volume the harder you play.

The compression also makes more sustain. Since the amp does a lot of compressing on its own in hard playing, there's not that much need for more of it in recording or mixing unless you want that—it all depends on the track and how it sits in the mix. If you want to add outboard compression, most compressors have adjustable attack and release settings, so these settings with guitar will affect your finger attack sound and your sustain.

What are your top five favorite guitar mics?

For distortion guitar, there's a reason why everyone goes right for an SM57, because it just about always works! There are a lot of quirky old oddball dynamic mics out there that work great on guitar. For tamer tones, I like just about any ribbon mic matched with the right preamp. The Neumann U 67 and the Sony C-37 are my favorite tube condenser mics for guitar.

What are your top five favorite mic preamps?

I don't want to make this a gear endorsement so I won't name any brands here. I've studied and done extensive shootouts on many different mic pres, and I have both a tube and a solid-state preamp prototype design I'm working on putting into production. If I told my opinion here of what I don't like, most would disagree.

I've had a change of heart on all the revered brands. So much of it is overrated. I've found that manufacturers' specs don't correlate very well to how good something actually sounds. Something with very good measurement specs can sound totally mediocre and unrealistic. There are other measurements that never get listed that do affect the sound, notably phase shift and square wave response.

I prefer the sound of a transformer-based mic pre, but it can't ring, and the phase shift has to be good. Ringing is a resonance peak that you can see on a scope with a square wave. It usually sounds very sibilant and harsh in the 4k region. Put some classic, way-overpriced preamps through this test, and you'll see what I mean. Some use inferior transformers that ring a lot and have really bad phase shift. Phase shift smears your top and bottom frequencies.

I'm not partial to tube or solid state when it comes to mic pres. A lot of tube designs I hear are too dark and tubby sounding; others can sound harsh and sibilant. Same goes for solid state. It all boils down to the design. How the different microphone types and preamps interact with each other is also a big factor—it's like how different guitar amps and guitars interact. It's all very subjective, so use your ears and pick what you like.

For guitar amps, how do tubes play a big part in a particular sound as opposed to solid state?

Tubes distort much differently than transistors. When transistors or IC chips clip, they dramatically chop off the waveform like a buzz saw, which turns a sine wave into a square wave. It's a very buzzy sound with pure odd harmonic distortion products, but this can be desirable for certain tones. Most fuzz pedals do this. A transistor or opamp is usually clean right up to the clipping point, and then the distortion turns on instantly like a switch. It's either 100 percent clean or 100 percent dirty—there's not much in between.

Tubes have a more gradual onset of clipping that doesn't chop the wave so abruptly—especially single-ended triodes as in the preamp stages of most guitar amps, which have asymmetrical clipping, which makes even harmonic distortion. Asymmetrical clipping is when only one crest of the wave gets cut off. Even harmonics are perceived as more musical. That's why tubes make for a smooth transition from clean to dirty that you can ride with the dynamics of your playing.

Solid-state amps work well for clean-only playing. Bass players often prefer a solid-state amp with a lot of headroom, like a high-power MOSFET amp. Some of those amps can be hybrid with a tube preamp and a MOSFET power stage. That way, you can play really loud onstage with some even harmonic tube coloration but still have lots of clean headroom. There's also the tube versus solid-state rectifier, where a tube rectifier will compress your amp more when you play hard, whereas a solid-state rectifier will give a tighter response.

Why change tubes and how often?

Tubes wear just like tires on a car—the harder and farther you drive 'em, the shorter they last.

What is the difference of the preamp stage, the power output stage, and the rectifier stage? What is each function?

The preamp stage is where the initial voltage gain happens. A guitar puts out a tiny AC voltage that needs to be amplified, and the preamp has a lot of gain. It makes a tiny signal much bigger. This is usually one or two stages that can be shared by a single tube, which is most often a 12AX7; it's a dual-stage tube.

In a Fender, the volume knob and tone stack are in between these two stages. In a Marshall, the channel volume is in between, but the EQ is after both. Then that can split out to a reverb driver and mix with the second channel followed by another stage or additional drive, like in a Mesa Boogie. Then it goes to a phase splitter or driver. The single-ended signal has to get split into two equal but out-of-phase signals that go to the pair or quad of power tubes in the output stage. This is where it makes the power necessary with the output transformer to drive the speaker. The rectifier is part of the power supply. AC comes from your wall outlet into the amp and goes into a power transformer, which steps up the AC into a higher AC voltage. Then it goes to a rectifier, which converts the AC into DC. That's raw DC that looks like a saw wave, which goes through a choke and series of filter capacitors to smooth it out to a straight DC line. Through this filter bank the DC is distributed to all the tubes stages in the amp.

Can you share any simple mods that can improve an amp's performance?

The simplest mod is to tube swap the very first preamp tube. Start a collection of 12AX7s and use your ears. This tube spot is where you'll hear the most appreciable difference between tube brands. Experimenting with different speaker types can dramatically change your tone. There are a lot of good speakers out there to choose from that could be a big upgrade to some of the stock cheaper speakers in a lot of newer amps. To use a tire analogy, this is like upgrading the factory tires on your car, which are usually good enough but kind of lame. Most people upgrade their tires if they want better performance from their car. This also applies to big production-run guitar amps. Unless it's a boutique or vintage amp, it probably has a crappy speaker and Chinese tubes in it.

What are some tips you can share with us for keeping an amp in optimum condition?

If it's vintage, take it to a reputable tech to have the capacitors replaced if it's never been done.

Store it in a dry environment; moisture and humidity cause oxidization on tube sockets and switches, and you don't want your paper speaker cones to get moldy. Not to mention the chrome chassis will rust and pit, and the Tolex will get funky and mildewy. Your guitar needs humidity; your amp doesn't! Keep it out of dusty areas and get a cover for it. And don't let mice get into it!

When you transport it, make sure the tubes are secure and won't fall out and get smashed. Some amps have tube retaining clips or locking tube shields, and some don't. Take each tube out and reinsert it a few times to work the socket clean. Any dirt buildup can cause a lot of awful noise.

What are your top five favorite recording amps? Why?

I think smaller, lower-wattage amps translate to bigger and better for recording with a close-placed microphone, as opposed to a 50+ watt amp and a big cabinet with lots of speakers. You can also get breakup distortion tone without blowing your head off, and you'll get a better signal-to-noise ratio in your recording signal chain. You can also more easily manage the bleed into other mics if you're recording live with other instruments in the same room.

So with that said, I like cathode bias amps 30 watts or less for recording: Fender Champ, Deluxe, Princeton, Vox AC30, all those quirky little Silvertone and Gibson amps. Magnetones are great for their vibrato. There are some really cool old tiny tube amps made by Kay that sound great. There are a ton of little boutique amps out there that borrow from these designs.

Shure-Fire Miking

When I was a kid growing up in New York, I remember that my dad had an old 1/4-inch four-track Grundig reel-to-reel tape recorder that was great for recording multiple guitar parts. I always thought it was so cool to sit in that sunroom and be able to hear the tracks played back, and to physically cut and edit the parts with a razorblade and edit block.

Today we have it so much easier. Whether you use a PC or Mac and any of the many programs out there, such as Cakewalk, Logic, Performer, or Pro Tools, editing has become a breeze. But the one true thing that has stayed constant throughout the years is recording great guitar tone.

Van Halen's first engineer, Donn Landee, used to get approached by fans asking him how he recorded Eddie's trademark guitar tone. He had to admit that he used a cheap SM 57 mic on a Marshall cabinet. As some of you readers may know, the Shure 57 is a basic $89 mic that you can purchase at any local music store. This proves that you can get great tone without breaking the bank.

What you need to understand are the various dynamics that come from both the guitar and the amp. For instance, when playing a Les Paul through a Marshall JCM800, you get a very compressed, overdriven rock tone as opposed to playing a Strat through a Fender Super Reverb, which produces a more dynamic blues tone. Both can be recorded successfully with an SM 57, but if you want to spend a little bit more cash, you can buy what I refer to as a "57 on steroids," the Sennheiser 421 mic.

If you have more of a budget and you want to capture the sound of your amp in the room, you may want to try the Neumann TLM 103 or the more expensive TLM 49, which are both large-diaphragm cardioid microphones. The large diaphragm of the mic will capture the ambience of the room. In particular, the TLM 49 has a wonderful airiness to its recordings. By comparison, the 57 has a very small mic diaphragm, which is more beneficial for unidirectional close miking.

I'm sure some of you have heard the buzz about ribbon microphones—and yes, it is true that in some recording applications of guitars, the ribbon mic is perfect for acoustic instrument replication. The Rolls Royce of ribbon mics is the Royer 121 or the famous Beatles BBC 4038. However, you can always go with the less expensive Beyerdynamic M160 mic and still get a great-sounding acoustic tone.

With any microphone you decide to go with, you'll have to experiment with placement techniques. Personally, I've had very good results recording acoustic guitars using the AKG C1000S, which I like to angle downward toward the fretboard side of the hole. Keep in mind that you may have to make some minor adjustments, depending on the size of the guitar body and your finger style.

I've been recording professionally for 17 years, and I am always trying to find new ways of achieving a great-sounding guitar tone. Just recently, I discovered a cool way to achieve stereo imaging by miking a single cabinet with two mics. First, close-mike one speaker between the cone and the edge with a Beyer M160 and far-mike the amp using a Neumann TLM 49 about five feet back, pointing the 49 directly at the Marshall insignia on the cabinet.

My baby is a Trident 32-channel mixing console, in which I use one of the mic pres for the Neumann and use the Universal Audio 610 for the M160. I buss them both to tape or Pro Tools and hard pan one left and one right. I've always found that experimenting with different mics and amps in combination with your guitar style can really produce that hot buttah tone!

2 From the Horse's Mouth: Gunslinger

What better way to get advice on recording than from the guitar heroes themselves? I tried to leave no stone unturned to get the real mojo from those I've admired through the years. What kind of special magic lies in the studio and what microphones and studio gear did they use? It became kind of a search for the Holy Grail, trying to uncover the secrets of recordings from the shredders. So I put together an impressive list of guitar slingers who generously shared their wisdom of recording secrets.

Jeff Beck in the Studio

No single word can describe the illustrious and diverse career that guitar icon Jeff Beck has enjoyed for the past half century. The quintessential guitarist's guitarist, he has received the Grammy Award for Best Rock Instrumental Performance five times. In 2009, he was inducted into the Rock and Roll Hall of Fame, presented by his old friend and former Yardbirds bandmate Jimmy Page. Beck's release *Emotion & Commotion* recruited the efforts of producer-engineer Steve Lipson. Steve has worked with numerous artists, including the Animals, Frankie Goes to Hollywood, Whitney Houston, Grace Jones, Jars of Clay, Paul McCartney, Pet Shop Boys, and Simple Minds. He produced Annie Lennox's first three solo albums.

Emotion & Commotion is a bit of a departure from the Jeff Beck we know from days past, when odd time signatures are met with screaming whammy-bar solos. Not surprisingly, Steve started out as an engineer for the Rolling Stones, soon becoming a protégé of Trevor Horn at ZTT. In the UK, there is a certain importance to working with Trevor Horn, which Steve has obtained and used very much to his advantage.

I had the pleasure of speaking with Mr. Horn's protégé about how one might go about recording an international guitar hero such as Jeff Beck.

> **How did you record the songs?**
> Probably everything I'm going to say is the worst-case scenario for those who are interested in recording. I used Pro Tools; we did everything individually and used the smallest, cheapest amplifier available, a Fender Pro Junior for about $400.

25

You captured his tone very well.

Yes, I think it comes from his fingers. In a way, he is not that bothered about big amps in the studio. He doesn't like big amps anyway, from what I can gather. He just plugged into the amp and said that it would do! And off we went.

What did you mike him with? Any particular favorites?

A Royer R-122V (Ribbon Microphone with Vacuum Tube Circuit and Military-Grade Tube) with a reflection filter screen. I close-miked the amp in the same room as us. (We didn't have a separate recording room.) We recorded the Royer through the Chandler LTD-2 straight into Pro Tools.

Did you record through a particular console?

No, I just have a bunch of outboard gear, Pro Tools, and an ICON D-Control surface.

Jeff Beck has always been an idol of mine. How was it working with such a guitar hero? Also, being the producer, did you have a large part in picking the songs?

It was brilliant working with him because he is an idol of mine as well. I worked with him years ago; we did music for a TV program that was a half an hour. Sitting three feet from him whenever he was playing was extraordinary. But after a while it's like anything else; you get past that, and you treat him like anyone else to get a good performance. Still, when I left the room and listened to what he did, it was magnificent!

It's funny—I'm a guitar player, and when I play something it sounds like rubbish, but when he plays the same thing it sounds unimaginable. I read a couple of reviews stating that he didn't stretch himself on the record. That remark is so ignorant it's hysterical. He stretched himself quite a lot on this record because the simplest things are the hardest things to play. He is the master of it! Like the opening piece, "Corpus Christi Carol"—the way he delivers those notes is amazing. They are simple notes that anyone could play, but nobody could play the emotion of those notes the way he does.

As far as song choices are concerned, it started with me telling him what I think he should do for the record. I gave him two CDs of songs, he listened to them, and he liked a handful. From that point we started to record. We started with a rhythm section, but it didn't work out. So Jeff and I went into a room and for the most part worked on the album. Then we got his keyboard player in, Jason Rebello, who had some song ideas, so the three of us put them together. Then we got Tal Wilkenfeld, the bass player, in to do her parts. Then lastly, we recorded the drummer and added a few bits here and there. There are only two tracks we recorded all together at once with the rhythm section.

Did you have vocalists in mind when recording the songs?

Jeff, his manager Harvey Goldsmith, and I thought there should be singing on the record. Imelda May had worked with Jeff in the past and was very up for doing it. Olivia Safe is an opera singer who hangs around at the studio, so she sang on some tracks. And Jeff knew Joss Stone, and she was up to it and came down and sang on two songs.

I see that Trevor Horn is listed as executive producer. What was his role in recording the album?

Trevor and I have worked together for more than 20 years. He gave us encouragement and helped with a couple of edits. The main thing was his encouragement really, because it was such a long process. Just making sure we're on track. After a while you get a little too close to things, so he was good at telling us, "It sounds good; keep going."

Did you go somewhere else to mix or did you use your own studio?

I used the same room. I have a big room, and I only use Yamaha NS-10s to mix on. I moved all my recordings into the box completely and utterly. The difference it would make to go out into a console and back is so esoteric. I think that would be focusing on the wrong things. There are more important things to focus on than that slight difference. Ninety-nine percent of the people would not be able to tell the difference if I mixed it through a Neve. The pros of mixing in the box are so huge by comparison.

Tell us about the choice of recording "Over the Rainbow."

Jeff has been playing that live for a while. We didn't choose it first because we were worried about the whole balance of the album. Originally, we thought it was a little bit too sweet. I was mixing the record, and Jeff was chopping some vegetables, and he chopped the end of his finger off on his left hand. It was stitched backed on, but it took a few weeks to heal. In the meantime, we had to do two songs, and "Over the Rainbow" was one of them. So he played it without using that finger. Unbelievable! It was his first finger, the anchor finger for a guitarist. He recorded the whole song without that finger.

What guitar did he use?

He used only one Fender Strat that he is used to, nothing unusual about it. It has a break in the neck that has been repaired, but he really isn't bothered by it. It's a sad lesson to us all. I didn't realize at the time, but what it states is that gear doesn't matter! It just doesn't matter at all.

I remember years ago, I was working with Paul McCartney, and I was engineering. He was producing Ringo Starr's solo album. It was a very interesting session. There was a moment when he said to Ringo, "Why don't you go sing the vocals?" Ringo said, "Yeah, and I want to sing into that microphone"—which was an old Shure Retro Styled Cardioid Dynamic, a rubbish mic. Paul said, "Certainly." While the assistant was setting up the mic with Ringo, I asked Paul if he wanted to set up another proper microphone. He said no. After the session I was speaking to Paul, and he said to me that the microphone doesn't matter, because it is all about the performance. If Ringo is happy singing into that mic, he will sing better and give a better performance.

What made you decide to go with the opera song "Nessun Dorma"?

There is a history to that. Jeff was playing Italy in some large venue last year, and someone suggested he perform "Nessun Dorma." He thought it was the most ridiculous idea in front of hundreds of thousands of people. But he stood up and played it, and the audience went ballistic. So he thought, "Let's just do it for the record," based upon this one gig.

To capture the tone he has live, the best thing to do is nothing. See, if you make a big deal about it, then he becomes conscious of it, and then there is a problem. The only discussion we had about the guitar tone was asking him to just give a bit more sustain at certain points. The way he addressed this is that he used the whammy bar to change notes without having to strike the string again. A lot of the times he finds the harmonic and hits it without fretting the note. This makes the note ring longer as opposed to fretting it. He is constantly changing pickups, using the volume control and the tremolo bar. He's always adjusting everything. Funny, he doesn't even know he's doing it. Amazing to watch from three feet away.

How did the orchestra come into play?

We went to a studio in north London where they record orchestras, where the engineer knows what he's doing. You can't be flaky with orchestras; it's not rock-n-roll, and you have to hit all on a certain time in the morning. All of the prep goes on before; it takes ages to get ready to record the orchestra.

There are two ways we did it. First, you have the orchestra record to the tracks already done, and the second, the orchestra records to a click because there is no rhythm. The latter is the tricky one. On tracks "Corpus Christi Carol," "Nessun Dorma," and "Elegy for Dunkirk" I had keyboardist Pete Murray come in and play with Jeff. Then I broke the song into beats in Pro Tools—in other words I had to put a click to Jeff and the keyboards because there is no beat behind them; it was very time consuming. So when Peter goes and conducts the orchestra, there is a click they can follow.

It's great advice for recording such a guitar icon: Let him do what he does best—play guitar! Steve admitted to me that he still has oodles of analog gear, but it's all in storage. He has successfully made the jump from the classic analog days to the full-fledged digital era. Many of us are envious of Steve's opportunity to sit only a couple feet away from the great Jeff Beck and experience in person the wizardry he possesses over the guitar. *Emotion & Commotion* is a culmination of Jeff's guitar voice and influence he has had on guitarists through the years.

Joe Satriani: Creating the Engine

Most people think of Joe Satriani as a shredder, but in fact he released an album back in 2000 entitled *Engines of Creation*, which blended electronica with rock guitar elements without losing that characteristic Satriani sound. Combining such disparate influences as Jeff Beck's *Who Else* and *You Had It Coming* with '90s electronica artists such as Apollo 440 and the Chemical Brothers, Joe was able to inject live rock guitar elements into electronic music.

On *Engines*, Joe takes some great jungle grooves—like the opening track, "Devil's Slide"—and blends them with synths and overdriven guitars to create a melee of contoured, driving tones. What Joe brings to the table is his great sense of melody and acrobatic finger stunts.

On the cut "Attack," Joe deftly matches the rhythm figure with the drum-n-bass groove, resulting in the perfect marriage of two genres typically thought to be incompatible. The tune "The Power Cosmic 2000, Part 2" aptly demonstrates Joe's sense of guitar work over funky loops and features a synth tone reminiscent of Jan Hammer's '70s fusion work. The chill track "Slow and Easy" infuses many textural layers of sitar and soundscape synth as Joe's melodic playing rides sweetly on top. All in all, this album exemplifies how guitar can intertwine perfectly within elements of electronica and still appeal to the guitar enthusiast.

Joe was gracious enough to take some time out of his busy schedule and answer a few questions about the album.

What inspired you to make an album of this style? Were there any particular artists or songs at the time that influenced you?

I enjoy making stylistic left turns with each recording project. *Engines* was the most radical of turns. I was getting into Boom Boom Satellites, the Prodigy, and the Crystal Method at the time and was dying to work my guitar into that kind of production style.

Did you use your home studio for this project or did you enlist an outside studio to track and mix?

Eric Caudieux and I recorded the record in his living room in Studio City. It was all Pro Tools and Logic Audio. There may have been a few stray guitar tracks from my home studio, but all the real creative work—recording and mixing—was done at Eric's.

Did you use digital or analog to record, and what was your setup?

I would plug my Ibanez JS1000 guitar into various pedals and into a variety of amp heads, then into a Palmer speaker simulator. Then I used a few different mic pres—Neves, V72s, et cetera. Sometimes we would aim for traditional sounds, other times not. Sometimes a plug-in would do the trick, and other times it's just all the pedals we found on the floor plugged in and turned up!

What pedals did you use on this project?

We had much success with the Moogerfooger pedals, the Fulltone Ultimate Octave, a DigiTech Whammy pedal, and a preamp called a Hafler Triple Giant.

Were there any in particular that really gave you that electronica feel?

The Hafler Triple Giant had the most robotic distortion, totally devoid of warmth and feeling. But, in the context of a song like "Borg Sex," it was perfect!

What mics did you use to record the guitar parts?

No mics, no speakers! We thought it was a cool thing at the time to make a record completely "in the box."

Do you have a favorite can't-live-without-it guitar processor that you used on this project?

It was most likely the SansAmp plug-in. I still enjoy using the SansAmp designs, both their plug-ins and rackmount preamps. Eric and I would use it here and there to spice guitar sounds up a bit. Sometimes, as in the song "Until We Say Goodbye," it was the guitar sound!

Billy Sheehan: Shy Boy at LaMoures

In the early '80s, I was a young musician growing up in New York City. I was walking to catch the train and the sweet smell of grit was rising from the pavement—when there used to be mysterious puddles of water on every street corner, even though it hadn't rained in weeks and the squeegee patrol was out, aggressively commandeering people's windshields at the Willis Avenue bridge.

I was on my way to LaMoures club to check out the band Talas and their incredible bass player, who was causing quite a buzz in the guitar community. Once inside, I staked out my little claim of space, had a cold brew—which I believe I had snuck in because I was underage—and waited. Like most of the crowd, I was skeptical of what kind of performance I was going to see, but that changed as the show began.

Talas was a great band with a lot of energy, but what I really witnessed was the best bass player I'd ever seen, even to this day. Lanky, longhaired, and dressed in spandex, the bass player ran out to center stage with his Fender P Bass and performed Eddie Van Halen's "Eruption." Most people couldn't perform "Eruption" on the guitar, let alone the bass—and in addition to performing two-hand tapping, he was doing acrobatics while playing to boot!

This man was Billy Sheehan, who would become a legendary bass player. Voted the Best Rock Bass Player five times in *Guitar Player* magazine's readers' poll, Billy earned a place in their Gallery of Greats alongside Jimi Hendrix, Paul McCartney, Geddy Lee, and Eddie Van Halen, to name a few.

Just recently, the B3 Tour was in town, and I caught Billy's performance with Jeff Berlin and Stu Hamm at B.B. King's on 42nd Street. I spoke with Billy after the show, and he agreed to play on a remake of the classic Jeff Beck song "Blue Wind" that I was recording.

I got the tracks in the mail, and they were stupendous. I'm an old two-hand tapping fool myself, and Billy played off the tracks I had given him and absolutely nailed it. I talked with Billy about recording "Blue Wind" and about his "Unleash the Beast" track on BHP Music's *Guitar Masters, Volume 1*.

What gear did you use on the recording of "Blue Wind"?

I used my home studio. I have an Ampeg SVT (turned way down!), as well as an Avalon preamp for direct sound. We recorded in Logic on a Mac. I used my regular bass that I play onstage—the Yamaha Attitude with RotoSound strings.

How did you record the bass?

We miked up the SVT cab, as well as split signals for a direct through a Radial Engineering direct box.

What format did you record the song on?

I'm all digital. We used Logic, Pro Tools, Digital Performer, and Cubase too, but I've been using Logic mostly. I use MOTU interfaces and a Yamaha 02R96 to route everything where it needs to go.

Give us a little background of your relationship to the classic version of "Blue Wind" with Jeff Beck and Jan Hammer.

I've jammed on the song since it came out many years ago. In many ways, Jeff really got the music scene going again with his releases in the '70s. *Wired* and *Blow by Blow* really ushered in a new era of improvisational jamming. I've recorded the song with Niacin, a B3 version that we perform live a lot. It's one of my favorite Jeff Beck songs—and there are many that I love.

What's your setup, bass, and amps that you used on the recording of "Unleash the Beast"?

It was done in the back room of a record company office in Tokyo, Japan, on bass and guitar PODs. We had no choice at the time; we needed another song for a single release, so we hustled this up. Sometimes being under pressure and having to make do with inadequate gear makes you work harder—I like the way it came out.

Are you currently working on a new project or album?

Yes, my third solo CD. I'm recording it in my home studio using my real gear. I'll also be doing a record with Tony MacAlpine and Virgil Donati, along with several other projects this summer—no rest for the wicked!

After working and talking with Billy, I can see why he's at the top of his field. He has a great attitude and is an absolute pleasure to work with. I think I speak for the entire guitar community when I say, "Thank you, Billy, for being such an inspiration throughout the years."

Steve Vai, the Bulgarian Blaze

On Steve Vai's 2006 release, *Real Illusions: Reflections*, he conquered new territory both rhythmically and sonically. One of the tracks that really caught my attention, both as a listener and a musician, was "Freak Show Excess," which features unusual rhythmic patterns derived from Eastern European music.

Steve says that one of his big influences is Bulgarian wedding music from the band Evo Papisov, and you can really hear it in the way he phrases the melody. Often, when artists interpret Eastern music, it sounds awkward and foreign. Steve is able to make it much more palatable to the Western ear. I had the pleasure of catching up with Steve to ask him about his recording techniques for the track.

What guitar and amps did you use for the "Freak Show Excess" recording?

I used a Carvin Legacy amp and an Ibanez Jem guitar.

Where do you record, and what programs do you use? Any special guests on the song?

All of my solo records are recorded in my home studio using Pro Tools. Billy Sheehan and Jeremy Colson were on this song.

What is your mic setup for recording the guitars?

If I remember right, most of the stuff is close-miked, but the change in pitch of the microphone gives the distinction. Also, EQ plays a vital role. I always keep a pair of C14s and a pair of 414s spread apart in the corners of the room. This is mixed into the sound at various levels depending on the desired effect. It's important to me to try and create a space for each guitar; the song should tell you what to do.

What kind of challenges did you encounter during mixdown? Did you use any special plug-ins or outboard gear?

It's a very dense, fast-moving track, so I didn't put many effects on it—it can get messy quick. I usually use Wave and Renaissance plug-ins for EQ and then compress analog before it hits the drive. I'm not a fan of digital compressors or reverbs. During mixdown, I usually use an L1 limiter plug-in. Before I decided to mix down internally and not come out analog, I spent a tremendous amount of time checking the mixdown phase using various formats.

I didn't listen to what people were saying on the best way to mix down regarding coming out of Pro Tools and going analog or digital to analog and back to digital, ad nauseam. Most people guess, or go on a hunch or a feeling, or just do what they heard someone else says is the best. I put my own ear to it, and frankly, I kept it in the digital domain. Going out to analog does not warm it up to me; I think that's an illusion. I don't know if all systems act similarly, but since I was using Pro Tools, I didn't go crazy trying different systems. The one thing I do with Pro Tools that makes a big difference is mixing down to two tracks through the stereo bus, instead of bouncing down. To my ear there is a big difference in the sound.

Are you currently working on a new project or album?

I had a new record out in July. It's called *Sound Theories*, and it was recorded live with the Metropole Orkest in Holland. I was commissioned to compose an hour of music by Holland's NPS (National Public Radio) for a cultural event. The show was broken up into two segments; the first part was pieces that I composed for the orchestra, and it doesn't include me on the guitar. The second half contained songs from my catalog that were arranged for the orchestra, and I played the guitar along with them. We recorded five concerts with them, and then I edited together *Sound Theories*.

I encourage all guitarists to check out "Freak Show Excess" and hear how Steve wonderfully articulates the melody through the track. To check it out, a quick search on YouTube will reward you with a video of Steve demonstrating his guitar techniques in this song.

Stanley Clarke: Bass in Your Face

Stanley Clarke was referred to as a legend by age 25. He is also a noted music composer, orchestrator, conductor, and performer for such films as *Boyz n the Hood*, *What's Love Got to Do with It*, *Passenger 57*, and *Poetic Justice*, to name a few. He has been quoted as saying, "Film has given me the opportunity to compose large orchestral scores and to compose music not normally associated with myself." Sony has even released a CD titled *Stanley Clarke at the Movies*, which showcases his true diversity as a musician.

In the 1970s he redefined and reshaped the way bass players approached their instruments. He took Larry Graham's (Sly and the Family Stone) slap-funk technique and pushed it to the next level. He's one of the renowned members of the progressive jazz-fusion band Return to Forever with Chick Corea. He is also the inventor of the piccolo bass and tenor bass. I had the pleasure of speaking with Stanley and asking him about the Larry Graham song "Hair," which he covered with Joe Satriani on the *Guitar Masters, Volume 1* compilation.

He shared the story of how he stumbled upon that particular song. "I think it was before they even recorded it. I was standing in a club in San Francisco with Carlos Santana. Carlos had on this trench coat with all these tape recorders underneath his coat—he's a real fan of music and loved to make recordings of live shows. He said, 'Man, you have to check out Graham Central Station.' It was in this little club. I knew Larry with Sly and thought he was an amazing bass player. When I heard 'Hair,' I said 'Oh, shoot!'" So as an homage to Larry, he recorded the song with Joe Satriani.

Stanley has a home studio where he does most of his solo projects for albums and film or television scoring. For the recording of "Hair," Stanley told me that he used his famous Alembic basses and F2 preamps. He recorded using two SWR amps and cabinets. One cabinet had 2 × 15-inch speakers, and the other cabinet housed 4 × 10-inch speakers. He then miked each cabinet separately and took a direct signal out of the amps themselves. This gave him the flexibility to blend during mixdown.

Stanley recorded using the Fairlight hard disk recorder, which at the time was similar to Pro Tools. Interestingly enough, he used an analog mixer to monitor and EQ the signal. During mixdown, his engineers still liked having something physical to work with and used the analog board. When mixing on digital hardware, such as Pro Tools, many old-school engineers like the feel of actual faders underneath their fingers to control the mix and utilize the onboard EQs. I have a vintage Trident 32 × 16 console, and the EQs are so musical that I want to be able to physically turn the frequency knobs to affect the tracks myself. It also allows me to bus certain tracks and use vintage outboard effects processors, such as the Eventide H3000 and the Lexicon PCM70.

As far as outboard gear, Stanley told me he is a fan of the Fairchild limiter, which he used on his first four solo albums. But with the new technology of today, there is a current Fairchild plug-in that Stanley feels gets 95 percent of the sound of the original hardware. He explained that because of the Alembic's wide dynamic range, you need a really nice limiter to control the sound when recording. This also affects Stanley's choice of mics; when choosing a mic, he considers not only the source, but the room ambience as well. For instance, when he wants a really big bass sound, he uses an outside studio. In the past he's used studios that housed separate rooms for each instrument, and he really likes the feel and sound of each instrument being physically separated.

With his new release *The Toys of Men*, he discussed the present state—or rather the lack—of instrumental music on the radio, saying, "The airplay thing is really tough—there is really nothing out there. I do have some faith in satellite radio. They have so many more possibilities and programs. All of my friends who have XM are musicians and are into the technology. As for the average guy, satellite radio just needs to figure out how to reach them and build up their listenership. Not until cars come with satellite-ready radio will it catch on."

It was a rare pleasure getting tips from the man who revolutionized the sound of the bass. I can only look forward to what lies ahead for this ever-evolving artist.

Will Ray-B-Bender Mojo

Recently, I had the pleasure of catching up with Will Ray, the renowned guitarist from the Helle-casters. For those who are not familiar with Will's work, the group's first album, *The Return of the Hellecasters*, became a hit with guitarists and earned them *Guitar Player's* Best Album and Best Country Album awards in 1993. In 1995, the Hellecasters recorded and released their second CD, *Escape from Hollywood*, and Hipshot products began marketing an invention of Will's called the Stealth Slide, in addition to the Will Ray-B-Bender model. Owing to the Hellecasters' popularity, Fender also released the limited-edition Will Ray Signature Jazz-a-Caster and the Custom Shop Will Ray Signature Mojo-Tele. The Hellecasters released their third album, *New Axes to Grind*, in 1998—on their own label, Pharaoh Records. Will released his first solo CD, *Invisible Birds*, in 1999, also on Pharaoh Records. He followed this with his second solo album, *Mojo Blues*, in 2000.

On *Mojo Blues*, he did a terrific interpretation of the folk song "Shenandoah." What is most striking about this instrumental piece is Will's wonderful tone and vibrato. The following is a Q&A of how he achieved that tone in the studio.

What guitars and amps did you use on the recording of "Shenandoah"?

The 1993 G&L ASAT Special and 1996 Fender Will Ray Mojo-Tele into a Carl Martin compressor, then into a Boss BCB-3 pedal board, which has an Ibanez TS5 Tube Screamer. From there the signal went into a first-year model Line 6 POD, where I had some kind of clean amp setting. I also took the recorded POD signal and played it into a miked Rivera M100 combo amp to beef things up. At mix time I used a little of each.

What format did you record the song on, analog or digital?

I recorded the basics—drums, bass, keyboards, and scratch guitar—on a Fostex G16 running at 30ips. It's a half-inch 16-track machine. After that I SMPTE synced it up with my Fostex D-160 digital hard drive recorder, and on the D-160 I did all my overdubs, which got transferred at the end of every day to the analog G16 machine as my backup. When it came to mixing, I usually used the tracks on the analog recorder instead of the digital ones, mainly to add a little warmth and mojo.

Give us a little background on the song and how you envisioned the guitar sounding.

This was a favorite song of me and my dad. When he died in 1996, I wanted to play it as a tribute to him. The Hellecasters were recording our third album at the time, and

"Shenandoah" was going to be on there, but at the last minute I decided to save it for my *Mojo Blues* album, which ended up being released a few years later.

The vibe I was looking for was a Roy Buchanan meets Mike Bloomfield kind of thing. I really loved the way Bloomfield and Al Kooper did *The Live Adventures of Mike Bloomfield and Al Kooper* version of Simon and Garfunkel's "59th Street Bridge Song (Feeling Groovy)," and I loosely based my intro on theirs. I would record my parts, later listening to what I did the next day with fresh ears. I just kept building upon what seemed to be working, while eliminating parts that didn't move me the next day. I'm a Gemini, and what sounds good to me one day may sound like rubbish the next. So, if a part on the recording sounded good two or three days in a row, it made it into the song.

There's a little taste of what goes into Will's tone. I know what you're thinking, and frankly, I was surprised as well that he made use of the Line 6 POD. It just goes to show that it is not always what you use but how you use it. Because he used the POD with a live amp, recording them both to analog tape, he got the best of both worlds, resulting in a clean and warm recording. God bless analog!

Randy Coven: Ace of Bass

I recently had the pleasure of doing a recording session with the renowned bass player Randy Coven, who's played with some of the best guitarists of our time, such as Steve Vai, Allan Holdsworth, and Yngwie Malmsteen, just to name a select few. Randy has an incredible background—he went to Berklee College of Music in Boston and was roommates with none other than the JEM 777 man himself, Steve Vai. They were in several bands together back in the '80s, and in fact Randy told me that he actually lent Steve Vai the money to make a phone call to Frank Zappa, which wound up getting Steve the gig of Zappa's musical transcriber. How's that for playing a hand in history?

I was familiar with Randy's work back in the day when the magazine *Guitar for the Practicing Musician* sported a cool record label called Guitar Recordings. They had some great releases, such as Randy's *Blues Saraceno* and the heavy metal violinist, Mark Wood. John Styx was the editor in chief at the time, and I got to know a lot of these guys.

So you can imagine, I was excited to work with Randy and had him come over to my new digs, Jungle Room Studios in New York. Fortunately, Randy doesn't live too far from the studio, so he was able to bring back with him two incredible basses that were handcrafted for him by Yngwie's guitar tech, as well as an Ashdown mini amplifier stack.

We started the session by placing the bass amp in the isolation booth. We miked the bottom cabinet that housed a 10-inch speaker with an AKG D 112, going to a channel on the Trident console. I know you're likely thinking, "Why is he recording a bass amp with a mic that is typically associated with recording a kick drum?" Simple answer: When the AKG is aimed toward the center of the speaker diaphragm, it captures the high frequencies that are radiated over a very narrow angle. It gives a fuller bass tone as well.

We also used a Radial J48 active direct box and took the signal of the bass itself to another channel on the console. Both signals were recorded down to analog tape, the trusty Ampex MM1200 24-track tape machine. By doing this, we were able to blend the two tones together when mixing—one track with the direct signal that complements the nuances of his graceful finger styles and the other track with the fat amp tone from the live miking. I always found that recording bass onto two-inch tape really fattens the bass sound and gives meaning to that old expression "tape saturation." Bass is a very subtle instrument when recording solo parts and takes a different approach compared to its six-string cousin.

One of the songs that we were recording was a funky rock piece. When it came to Randy's solo, it took a bit of time to find the right tone. We tried many different pedals, such as the Electro-Harmonix Deluxe Electric Mistress and a Tube Screamer, and different flangers, and we finally settled on the Electro-Harmonix Mini Q-Tron. The Q-Tron is a very versatile pedal with a cool envelope filter containing a high-pass and a low-pass mode that works well on bass. The high-pass filter helps the bass cut through a mix, especially when it comes to soloing. By setting the actual filter type, drive, and Q controls, you can actually get a vowel-sounding tone, which is great for funk guitar and bass. The colorful Bootsy Collins uses this quite a bit in his recordings. By using the Q-Tron in this manner, Randy's solo turned out to be very expressive.

I know guitarists are always on a quest to achieve tone. This is the same exact quest bass players are trying to conquer as well. Remember Stanley Clarke with Return to Forever, Billy Sheehan with Talas, and Stu Hamm with Joe Satriani? These bass players have awesome tone, so let's not forget our four-string friends. If you want to hear a sample of Randy's tone and performance, check out the song "I Wish," recorded with Zakk Wylde on the compilation *Guitar Masters, Volume 1*.

Andy Timmons: Creating Killer Tone

I recently had the pleasure of sitting down and speaking with Favored Nations' guitarist Andy Timmons to discuss the recording techniques used on the release *Resolution*. For those of you unfamiliar with Andy, he's a former member of the '80s pop-metal band Danger Danger. His other projects have included stints as Olivia Newton-John's music director and guitarist for seven years, as well as sharing the stage with Joe Satriani, Ted Nugent, and the Beach Boys—how's that for diversity? Andy spoke with us about his striking tonal control and masterful use of effects on his latest offering.

Could you describe the creative process involved in making *Resolution*?

It was quite the process of experimentation and discovery. It was the first record we ever approached strictly as a trio (Andy Timmons Band), and about halfway through we decided it would be nice to strip it down to just one guitar performance. Some of the basic tracks actually go back to 2001–02—on my previous Favored Nations album, *That Was Then, This is Now* we had recorded four new tracks. When we turned it over to [Favored Nations label owner] Steve Vai, he loved it. Steve liked hearing the fingers on the frets and the dynamics of everything, because it wasn't muddled up with other stuff going on. After he said that to me, I decided to do a whole record like that. From there I got really excited; I knew it was going to be a challenge, and it really proved to be a very interesting one.

What guitars and amps did you use for the recording?

A '68 Marshall Plexi Super Lead panned on one side of the stereo field and a '79 Marshall JMP panned on the other side. Believe it or not, this was the first time I had ever played through a Marshall amp. I played both of them simultaneously through a Framptone Amp switcher with my signature Ibanez AT300 and AT100 guitars, which enabled me to play both amps with one guitar loud and clean using a tape echo and tube driver in front. For the album's title track, I re-amped the Marshall through a Leslie 122 cabinet to get that swirling, Hendrix-y sound.

Mike Danne's role on this recording went beyond typical bass duties. Can you tell us more about his input on *Resolution*?

Mike was a major component on this record. We've played together for years, and he has a great ear for music—we're able to feel the push and pull from each other. He actually coproduced the album, going for a very natural feel by recording all the guitar tracks in his studio without using any EQ.

What are your favorite cabinets to use?

The Mesa Boogie 212 Rectifier cabinets; I find them to be very focused, fat, and warm sounding. My ears are so tuned to those cabinets and the Celestion Vintage 30 speakers.

Could you tell me more about the mics and format you used to record the album?

Most of the takes were one pass through on the same rig. I used all SM57s for recording the guitar. We recorded all the basic tracks onto two-inch analog tape in an old Neve room just south of Dallas, and then we bounced to Pro Tools, then to Logic to record the guitar tracks, bouncing everything back to Pro Tools for the final mix. We wanted something unaffected.

I found Andy's approach very interesting because it demonstrates an old-school way of thinking in which you do not rely on EQ from the mixer or outboard gear. Instead, you reposition mics or adjust the tone of the initial source to get the desired recording. Also, a good point is that you don't necessarily need expensive mics to capture great tone. The Shure SM57 microphone is one of the most affordable mics on the market, but it's very effective for capturing electric guitar tones.

Another great aspect of Andy's recording is the use of the Framptone Amp Switcher, available from www.robertkeeley.com. I have one myself, and it really enables you to get a stereo-like guitar image and texture using two different amps. You can simultaneously record extreme amps, such as a Fender Super Reverb and a Marshall JCM800, and use different effects on each amp. For instance, I used a Tube Screamer for the Fender Super Reverb and a Uni-Vibe through the JCM800 and hard panned each amp left and right. It's important to note that you can accomplish this by doing several recording passes using different guitars and amps, much like the classic 1992 Alice in Chains album *Dirt*, produced by Dave Jerden. Layering various guitars and amps will give you a fatter and richer tone for rhythm tracks. However, when doing melodies and solos, the amp switcher is a more accurate way to record two amps at once.

Doug Stapp: Dr. Frankenstein

I don't know if many of you are familiar with Texas shredder Doug Stapp, but once you hear his remake of Edgar Winter's "Frankenstein," you'll become an instant fan. Together with Shrapnel recording artist Scott Stein, they created a guitar-centric arrangement of Edgar's '70s rock classic. Michael Molenda, editor of *Guitar Player* magazine, says, "Headbangers can get off on Doug's killer version," and *20th Century Guitar* magazine calls it "spot-on." Not bad for an up-and-coming guitarist. One of the great things about this explosive, in-your-face rendition is that it was all done live. Before recording, Doug had never played with Scott or the drummer, but when the guys got together in the studio, they were able to bang out the track in just three takes. What's also great about this version is that you can really feel the energy of the live performances and hear how well Scott and Doug harmonize together. I caught up with Doug to chat about the recording of the song.

What was your setup—guitars, amps, et cetera—for the recording of "Frankenstein"?

I used a Carvin Legacy amp and an Ibanez Jem guitar.

How did you record the guitar?

Well, 95 percent of the track was recorded live. I think there were only a couple of rhythm overdubs and a couple of minor miscue fixes on guitar. Scott's cab was in an iso booth with one SM57 off-axis and a ribbon mic. My cab was in a hallway of the studio with one SM57 off-axis and a ribbon mic. I can't remember where the ribbons were set—it was a pretty "live" mic job, though, and the amps were super loud.

What format did you use to record the song—analog or digital?

We recorded and mixed the whole session in about six hours, completely in Pro Tools. The studio we used was loaded down in current Pro Tools gear, and the engineer was amazing. He really knew what we were looking for.

Give us a little background of the song and how you envisioned the guitar sounding.

The background actually goes back many years. Scott was a big influence on me when I was a teenager—I first met him when my band opened for Haji's Kitchen, and he was their guitarist. They did an amazing version of "Frankenstein" on seven strings that night, and it just blew me away. That version was originally a version that was written by Scott and Derek Taylor when they had the band Tommy Lamey. If I'm not mistaken, in the early '90s Derek first had the idea to do a crazy version of the song for a show they were opening.

Fast-forwarding quite a few years later, I emailed Scott to see if we could do that version for my new record, and thank God, he agreed. We decided to keep the song a bit more like the original but add our own flavor on top. Putting sax, guitar, and keyboard parts between two guitar players in harmony was a blast, and I have to thank Scott, Derek, and the Haji's guys for putting the idea in my head to redo this amazing song and of course thank Scott for arranging the whole thing. The take you hear is the third take, 95 percent live in the studio. We were looking for a big, raw feel, and we got exactly what we were looking for—thanks to great engineers.

The creation of "Frankenstein" in the recording laboratory would garner even Mary Shelley's approval. Check out Doug's work on *Guitar Masters, Volume 1*, available at record stores and online.

Eric Johnson's NASA Tone

The man who needs no introduction to the world of guitar and outstanding tone: Eric Johnson. The first time I heard Eric was back in 1985, when he did a guest appearance on Steve Morse's solo record *Stand Up*. He contributed vocals on the song "Distant Star," in addition to his signature guitar tone. The following year, *Guitar Player* magazine showcased Eric's song "Cliffs of Dover" on their promo vinyl record that came with every issue. Spinning that song for the first time on the record player had a very powerful effect on me and prompted me to see him at the China Club in New York the very same year. He put on an amazing show, and I felt as if I had witnessed a great guitar player before he really exploded onto the scene.

Four years later, "Cliffs of Dover" earned Eric a Grammy for Best Rock Instrumental, topping fellow nominees Allman Brothers Band, Danny Gatton, Rush, and Yes. Even before this song gave him the recognition he deserved, he had been a session player in the '70s for such artists as Cat Stevens, Carole King, and Christopher Cross. In fact, Eric had played on the Grammy-sweeping Christopher Cross self-titled album in 1980. Since then Eric has released several solo CDs, one in particular in 2005 entitled *Bloom*.

The History of "Columbia"

I had the pleasure of talking with Eric about his CD *Bloom* and the song "Columbia." For me, that song in particular felt like the CD's signature song due to its "Cliffs of Dover" vibe as well as its positive, upbeat progression. Eric has a keen sense of songwriting and composition, and that has always placed him head and shoulders above other guitarists, hence his Grammy Award, which is rare for a rock instrumentalist.

When I caught up with Eric and asked him about the origin of the song, he said he wrote it in memory of the space shuttle *Columbia*, which had disintegrated in 2003 over his home state of Texas less than half an hour before its scheduled landing. Being a born and bred New Yorker, I could relate to his need to express himself over such a devastating tragedy hitting so close to home. Eric told me that he had always been a fan of astronomy and NASA, so when the tragedy took place he immediately felt compelled to sit down and write a song commemorating the lives that were lost. Eric said, "I wanted to make it more of a positive message, a salute, a celebration rather than just concentrating on a few moments of tragedy, but instead the bigger picture of these brave people's lives." After the song was released, he mentioned that crew member Kalpana Chawla's husband contacted him to say that he, along with other astronauts at NASA, really enjoyed the song because it was an uplifting tribute instead of a dirge.

Setup and Gear for *Bloom*

Eric's typical setup is a BK Butler Tube Driver or an AC Booster through a Marshall JMP Super Lead and a Dunlop Dallas Arbiter Fuzz Face or an old Ibanez Tube Screamer through a Marshall JTM45. "I have a couple of different Marshalls with a little different circuitry. Some are more Hendrix rhythm, big, Fender-sounding, and not as grainy, with bigger, thicker rhythm tones and overdrive. Then I have some that are more Super Lead JMP that have a lot of gain within the amp. I'll crank that up and get a lot of distortion from the amp. I also have a Twin Reverb that has Eminence speakers. When you crank it up, it has an interesting type of lead tone."

For the song "Columbia," Eric used a Strat with the Butler Tube Driver through a JMP Marshall. Eric will sometimes use two amps at a time with a switcher to get a stereo effect, but when overdubbing he likes to concentrate on one amp at a time. He says that the BK Butler works really well with the Marshall. It was nice to talk to an artist who really writes from the heart and has true meaning behind his compositions. Check out Eric's genius on *Bloom* from Favored Nations, as well as his latest release, *Up Close* (2010).

Tommy Emmanuel: Finger-Picking Licks

Native Australian guitarist Tommy Emmanuel's technique has been described as fingerstyle, a unique way of playing the guitar similar to the way a pianist plays piano using all 10 fingers. In fact, guitar legend Chet Atkins honored Tommy Emmanuel with the title of "Certified Guitar Player" for his lifetime contribution to the instrument, a rare honor shared by only three other people in the world—Jerry Reed, Steve Wariner, and John Knowles.

His career has spanned more than four decades and includes 20 albums. Among his achievements was receiving a 2007 Grammy nomination for the song "Gameshow Rag" from his CD, *The Mystery*, which was released on the Favored Nations label. Tommy was also voted one of the Top Three Favorite Artists in an *Acoustic Guitar* magazine readers' poll. Tommy was honored by Australia's *Rolling Stone* magazine as most popular guitarist for two consecutive years. He also has four Platinum and Gold albums and garnered the Golden Guitar award in both 2006 and 2007 at the CMAA Awards in Australia.

Ironically, back in the mid-1990s, Tommy and I had something in common: NAC Radio. I had signed with Instinct Records and just released my acid jazz album *Last Kiss Goodbye*, which received quite a bit of airplay at NAC Radio. Around that same time, Tommy's CD *Midnight Drive* was cruising the same stations on the dial. Oddly, we had never spoken until this interview.

I asked him about his most recent CD, *The Mystery*, and in particular, the song "Cantina Senese."

What guitars and mics were used to record the CD?

In "Cantina," I played three parts, sometimes in unison and sometimes in harmony. I used my maple guitars and miked them with two Neumann 149s. I got a drum machine to play the bass drum and conga parts, then overdubbed brushes and real drums around it. Two of the guitar parts were played on steel strings, with one panned to the left and one panned to the center. The third part was played on a very ordinary Takamine nylon string that I borrowed. I wanted to get the sound of a real guitar trio with a party atmosphere.

Where was the album recorded?

At a friend's place in Nashville called Azalea Studio and mixed at Wistaria Studio in Virginia. Kim Person engineered the album—she is a great engineer, specializing in acoustic guitar. She can get such a great natural sound from the guitar.

What acoustic miking techniques did you use?

I used a Neumann KM 184 pointing down the neck of the guitar toward the sound hole. Right in front of me, I used a handmade mic that a friend of Kim's had designed, similar to an old Telefunken 251 and centered to the sound hole about eight inches in front of me. I also took a direct out from my guitar pickup into my AER acoustic amp that was miked in a separate room. When we did the mix, we left both acoustic guitar mics dry and put just a little reverb on the amp mic to create that big, beautiful depth—that really crystal-clear sound, like you're right in front of my guitar.

What preamps were used?

Kim used Pendulum preamps, which were made for her studio. [Pendulum Audio specializes in high-quality, hand-built vacuum tube recording equipment designed for amplifying stringed instruments—check them out at www.pendulumaudio.com.]

Digital or analog?

We recorded the whole album in three days using Pro Tools. For preproduction, Kim goes into the studio the day before and sets up the mics and tweaks the sounds, so everything is ready for me to record. The next day, I find the right spot on the mic and just go from there. I like using my custom guitars that were made for me in Australia.

Marcus Nand: Shredding the Rumba

How many of you remember a band called Freak of Nature, formed by ex–White Lion singer Mike Tramp in the early '90s? It wasn't a very memorable hair band and was nothing spectacular in the music department, but it spawned a talented guitarist from Spain named Marcus Nand.

Nand was born into a musical family in England and started playing the acoustic guitar at the age of seven. When he was eight, his family migrated to southern Spain. At the age of 12, he started playing semiprofessionally in venues in the province of Malaga, and he later learned and played flamenco guitar with the Gypsies of Andalucia—a privilege reserved for few outsiders. With his unique background, he moved to Los Angeles to pursue his love of music and has since played with Jeff Scott Soto, Carmine Rojas, and Neal Schon, to name a few. He also performed on the Terry Bozzio, Tony Levin, and Steve Stevens album *Situation Dangerous*.

What is most striking about Nand's playing is his very fluid, classical acoustic feel. He first got in touch with me when I was producing *Guitar Masters, Volume 1* through Seymour Duncan. Nand's style is very reminiscent of the Gipsy Kings—when it comes to flamenco guitar, he plays with confidence and authenticity. The song he sent me was "Rumba," and I immediately knew that it would be a perfect addition to the compilation.

What guitars and amps did you use to record "Rumba"?

I used a Takamine nylon string cutaway, a Godin Grand Concert, and a '57 reissue Strat with a Seymour Duncan little '59 mini-humbucker in the bridge. The Strat is so used that it actually looks like a real '57. It's still my favorite guitar, though. I used the Takamine for the flamenco "rumba" rhythms, the Godin for the main melody, and the Strat for the lead.

How did you capture the guitars and amps?

The flamenco "rumba" rhythm needed to sound organic. The only way to really do that is to mike a real nylon string or flamenco guitar. It takes me ages to get a guitar sound, so I just move the mic around until it's right. I have no technique for that—it's really just trial and error. I doubled the rhythms and hard panned left and right to get that fat, Gipsy Kings–type of sound. You can actually quadruple track that type of rhythm to make it sound great, especially if the takes are loose and there is space in the track. Then, I sent them to a group track and compressed the group.

The melody was a little simpler. The Godin guitar has a great preamp, so it's relatively easy to make it sound good. It's also the type of nylon string that sounds good with a pick, so that's what I did. I just used the XLR out and went straight in and compressed. EQ-wise, I find if you take around 1.5k out of pretty much any direct guitar signal, it makes it sound a little more natural.

I used to be a tone junkie and always used Marshalls straight and modified—and still do live—but I've found that for home recording, the Line 6 amps and POD do the trick. I used the POD straight in for the electric guitar tone on the solo.

What format did you use to record the song?

The song was recorded entirely on hard drive using Steinberg Cubase SX3.

Give us a little background of the song and how you envisioned the guitar sounds.

The song came about because I was doing some tests for an upcoming project. I wanted something not to showcase my guitar playing, but to be a melodic, image-evoking experience for the listener. Well, I guess I wouldn't have minded it showcasing my playing, too! I guess I wanted to do something with commercial appeal.

There are many aspects to my guitar playing that I can't always use in the same track. With "Rumba," I wanted to do something with all those aspects, such as flamenco rhythm, some cool lead playing, and electric guitar. I always try for textures when recording guitars, and I'm a firm believer in the right tool for the right job, but sometimes it's hard to combine nylon string and electric. I actually enjoy doing that and wrote a whole vocal record of [nylon string] combined with electronic instruments, which I'll finish one of these days.

Howard Hart: Majestic Touch

California-based guitarist Howard Hart packs a huge punch with fat guitar licks and great production. Seymour Duncan actually got me hipped to Howard when I was putting together *Guitar Masters, Volume 1*. I was really impressed with his guitar style, but even more so with his innate ability for production. He has a great ear for instrument placement in a mix, which is very important for instrumental music, so I immediately approached him to be part of the BHP Music compilation *Get the Led Out!* He fittingly chose "Four Sticks" for the project.

What guitars and amps did you use to record "Four Sticks"?

The main guitar I used was an EVH Wolfgang, but a couple of the rhythm bits were doubled using the Ibanez RG series. There are also some acoustics scattered throughout the mix as well—an Ovation steel string and a Montalvo nylon. I like layering guitar tones. A little goes a long way in terms of subtle differences in gain and bite. This particular track was done with a combination of a Mesa Boogie DC-3 and a Genesis 1—I actually love that thing for adding a little edge to the mic sound. The cabinet used was a Mesa with two 12-inch Celestions—the Vintage 30s.

Do you have your own studio or did you use an outside studio? Were there any key players involved in making this song?

I used my own studio that's set up at home. What's funny about this track is that I had just returned from my honeymoon and was a little crunched for time, so I recorded the drums at a friend's studio, and we used Pro Tools. When we brought the tracks back, there were a few problems, and I had to put some extra time in to straighten it all out. I used bits from the Pro Tools session, and everything else was done at the home studio.

Everyone involved really put in 100 percent. Nick Sitar played drums and also came over to the studio to do the battery of percussion. Melisa Kary was key because she offered up a lot of great ideas during the recording process and helped out enormously with coproduction. Rod Ratelle played bass and came up with the idea of using an upright acoustic-electric on the track—I wish you could hear more of it. It was great, but with all those guitars and the wall of percussion, the subtleties sometimes got lost. The vocal "ahs" on the B and C sections were an afterthought. It just felt like it needed something, so I asked Melisa, and she made it happen. She's done a lot of work in the past with producers like Michael Walden and really knows how to record and layer vocals. It's a two-part harmony (keeping with Page's concept), but we did two or three per line—it was a lot of fun building the beast.

How did you record the guitar?

Believe it or not, I still love a Shure 57 for guitar. Close-miking is cool for certain things, but I actually like to back off the amp a bit—maybe four or five feet back and up a bit. Boogies and Marshalls sound good loud, but you have to worry about the "studio ghosts" that day, so they can actually be captured. I've recently been going through some old DAT tapes and doing a little re-mastering. There's nothing like a great-sounding amp in a great-sounding room with all that breath being caught by the microphone.

What format did you record the song on?

The original drum tracks were done on Pro Tools. Everything else was done using SONAR, but as usual, I like to approach things with a tape mentality, in terms of performance. At this point in time, hard drive recording is incredible—but it still comes down to the musician. Rod did his bit straight through, with one punch to tighten up a kick. I like that because I believe you can feel it on a track, but I'm a digital man at this point.

Give us a little background of the song and how you envisioned the guitar sounding.

"Four Sticks" is an all-time favorite for me, and, in my strange head, it has always sounded like an instrumental. Because of this, it seemed a cool choice for the Bohemian project. Page is always "touchy" territory; he was brilliant in the studio, and his body of work speaks for itself. As far as envisioning the guitar sounds, I think what we hear in our head is always grander than the final outcome, but that's just being neurotic! I'm pleased with this track, and it was great fun to do. The solo section was interesting.

It was late, and I played four or five solos, so I just picked one. The next day it didn't grab me, so I got the idea of "orchestrating" it—dropping in harmonies, kicks, et cetera, throughout the take—and it worked. It's actually one of my favorite sections in the track—happy accidents!

Steve Morse on Cruise Control

Having been a Steve Morse fan since his solo projects, *The Introduction* and *Stand Up*, I was curious to learn that he was working with a new artist. Known for his blazing guitar riffs and instrumental sensibilities, Steve has ventured into uncharted waters by teaming up with singer-songwriter Sarah Spencer on her latest album, *Angelfire*. Being a hardcore instrumental guitarist, I was skeptical about a guitar hero joining forces with a folk-pop singer. But having listened to the CD thoroughly, I can say that it's well produced, and Steve's style is very evident. It's nice to hear the softer side of Steve contained in the CD's ethereal passages.

I caught up with Steve to talk about this fresh project and other music news.

What guitars and amps did you use to record *Angelfire*?

I started with my normal Music Man electric. Then I used a Buscarino acoustic-electric nylon string guitar, an Ovation steel string, a Steinberger 12-string, a Music Man baritone guitar tuned down to B, and a Line 6 Variax. Everything was either miked or direct.

What studio did you use to record your parts?

I used my own studio. It's a very modest endeavor, built for space rather than sonic perfection. I'm attached to my old board, which is still wired to my old Studer 24-track, so everything went through the board on its way to being recorded by the computer. The old Urei compressors still work and are used on all vocals and clean guitars.

How did your guitar approach with Sarah Spencer differ from your solo productions?

My approach is always the same: to try and create sonic depth. With *Angelfire*, I wanted to have no distortion at all while she was singing since her voice is so perfect, which meant combining different sounds that were clean. For instance, while I'm playing a busy arpeggiator part on the nylon string, I might add a 12-string to double only the notes that are on the fifth and sixth strings, to accentuate and slow down the apparent density of what sticks out to your ear. So instead of hearing a lot of equal volume notes, there is a constant harmonic backdrop of arpeggios with a more sparse, ringing 12-string—just loud enough to notice the difference.

The material itself pushes you in a certain direction. For example, in the tune "Omnis Morse Aequat," the clean guitars are being wah'ed by rolling the tone control with my little finger instead of using a wah pedal. This gives the effect of unearthly brass and string accompaniment when it's mixed right, which fits the stately nature of the tune. In "Get Away" the riff was crying out to be played on the baritone guitar, since it's in a key that seems too high for standard tuning without distortion. The baritone with a clean sound gave it a slightly unusual framework.

What format did you record the songs on?

I used Cubase SX1, 2 and 3; it's very powerful and works well for me. I find the German approach easy to understand and remember, only after years of frustration. All software like this requires quite a ramp-up period of time to learn what to do. Basically, you have to be able to edit almost everything on the fly or have a superhuman memory and "fix it later." With Sarah, I simply had to decide which take sounded better and keep it. There were literally three notes of hers that I fixed, so we ran no pitch correction, which kept it natural.

What pedals did you use on this project?

I don't think I used a single foot pedal, but I usually don't in the studio. One technique I used was a doubling effect—say, a chorus delay on the opposite side of the dry part. Then when doubling, pan the doubled part exactly opposite so that on take one, you have dry on the left, effect on the right, and then on take two, they flip-flop. It makes it sound sonically complex without totally phasing out. The doubles need to be pretty close to make that work, since it's best if they are the same volume.

What other upcoming projects or albums are you working on?

I played on a track called "Towers," to be featured on the album *Brian Tarquin Presents: Fretworx*, which benefits the Friends of Firefighters. The Steve Morse Band is also finishing up a new studio album, somewhat in the style of Southern Steel, and I recorded demos of my son's two bands, Haneda and Dose of Reality, which they instantly published on their MySpace pages.

Robin Trower: *Seven Moons* Tone

Robin Trower, the iconic disciple of Hendrix, was born on March 9, 1945, in Catford, South East London, England. Catford is a town within London located at the heart of the London Borough of Lewisham, dating back to Saxon times and having a rich artistic history. So it is no surprise that it would be the birthplace of one of the most talented and tone-respected guitar heroes of our time.

In the early turbulent '60s, Robin formed a group that would come to be known as the Paramounts, later including fellow Southend High School mate Gary Brooker. The Paramounts disbanded in 1966 to pursue individual projects. Trower then joined the band Procol Harum in 1967, staying until 1972. In 1973 he teamed up with bass player James Dewar and drummer Reg Isidore to form the Robin Trower Band.

Without a doubt, Trower's most famous album is *Bridge of Sighs* (1974). A former Procol Harum bandmate, organist Matthew Fisher, produced the album. In 1980 Trower teamed up with former Cream bassist Jack Bruce and drummer Bill Lordan for the magnificent self-titled release *B.L.T.*, an outstanding retro Hendrix experience. Now they are back for their first collaboration in years with the release of *Seven Moons*. Trower's heavy univibe guitar tone can be heard meshing with the distinctive voice of Jack Bruce.

I had the pleasure of interviewing Robin as he came off tour with his reincarnation of *B.L.T.*, in which Gary Husband replaces Bill Lordan on drums.

What's your setup, guitar, and amps that you used on the recording of *Seven Moons*?

I used two Cornell Plexi 18/20 amps—these are the 20-watt 1 × 12 combos. I would split from my pedals, running one clean and one more overdriven. On the track "Just Another Day," I used my DejáVibe going through one amp and the other straight. My pedals were a Fulldrive II and a Clyde wah, both by Fulltone, as is the DejáVibe. The guitar was my signature model Stratocaster from the Fender custom shop, built by Todd Krause. This model is really quite a vintage-type Strat (saddles) with a '70s neck with large frets and locking tuners. I thought the larger headstock might possibly give the guitar a bit more resonance. The neck pickup is a '50s reissue, the middle is a '60s reissue, and the bridge pickup a modern winding for more oomph.

Do you have your own studio or did you use an outside studio for this project?

I do not have my own studio, and for *Seven Moons* we went to a studio in London called Intimate Studios. I recommended it to Jack because I like the acoustics in the room: wooden floor, not too dead—very good for guitar and drums.

I was a very big fan of the original *B.L.T.* album, and it was great to see that you and Jack are back for another collaboration. How much did Jack Bruce play a role in both composing the album and production?

I would come to Jack with a guitar idea and a lyric, and he would turn it into something great. All the songs are cowritten. We both acted as producers on the sessions but I always let Jack choose the take. If he was happy, I was happy. I did a lot of the guitar soloing on my own, and then Jack would come in and do his vocals. One day he sang five master vocals in a few hours—amazing!

How did you record the guitar—mics, room amp, or close mic, et cetera?

A Shure 57 a few inches from each combo.

What format did you record the songs on? Analog or digital? Can you be specific about tape players, such as Ampex, or digital formats, such as Logic, Pro Tools, et cetera?

Seven Moons was recorded on tape through a Neve VSP 72 with Flying Faders to an Otari MTR90 (two-inch 24-track analog) and mastered to a MCI JH-10 (half- to quarter-inch analog mastering).

Being a guitarist, I'm curious about what foot pedals you used on this project. Were there any in particular that really gave you that classic Hendrix feel? Perhaps you can share a technique with the readers?

Fulltone Fulldrive II, Clyde wah, and a DejáVibe. I am very flattered that you think I have something of the Jimi Hendrix feel. All my influences were black Americans, blues, rhythm and blues, and soul. Of course Jimi Hendrix was the first guitarist to pull all of these threads together.

What upcoming projects or albums are you working on?

Jack and I are trying to do some dates in Europe in the New Year—hoping to have one show filmed.

I knew when I heard this release that it was recorded properly onto tape. It's so refreshing to see artists still using this format. It's tried and true! Just check out the tracks "Lives of Clay" and "Bad Case of Celebrity" to feel those dynamics in the recording. Of course, its Robin's playing that comes through with soulful blues, the way only he can do it, but the tape is a living, breathing integral part of the recording. *Long live analog tape!*

Chris Mahoney: Whole Lotta Guitar

New York guitarist Chris Mahoney sent me his self-released CD, *Rebirth*, about a year and a half ago. Though just a pup in the guitar scene, his debut displayed a wonderful understanding of melody and dynamics, which led me to ask this talented player to be involved in the Led Zeppelin salute CD, *Get the Led Out!* His spirited cover of "Whole Lotta Love" captured the essence of Zeppelin and became the first track on the CD.

Chris has been honing his chops just 70 miles north of New York City, in a sleepy town called Poughkeepsie, and has opened up for such acts as Al DiMeola, Steve Vai, Gov't Mule, and Blue Oyster Cult.

What's your setup, guitar, and amps that you used on the recording of "Whole Lotta Love"?

I used my Terry McInturff DRP Taurus, which is basically a customized Taurus. Terry's guitars are amazing. I've got four of them, and there simply is no reason to play anything else. They are the most resonant guitars I've heard. As far as amps, I used the Soldano SLO 100. This is the setup I've been using for a few years now. The Soldano is the most honest of all the amps I've tried. The SLO really lets a guitar breathe and is so responsive. For effects, I used an Eventide Eclipse for the lead lines. It was a ducked delay as to texture the vocal line of the track, yet not be too much. For the breakdown part, we went a bit beyond using some reverse guitar effects and tempo-based tremolo effects. I used a Vox wah on the solo in the up position to separate the solo breaks. I was looking to have a big mood shift in the segments musically as well as sonically, so we did the lines in an alternating pattern—the straight sound followed by the wah sound, panning each one hard left and right. It kind of has that call-and-answer vibe.

Tell me about the studio you used and the players who were involved in making this song.

I have a small studio where I do all my programming, but for drums and guitars I recorded the track at Galuminum Foil studios in NYC with producer Chris Cubeta, who also happened to play drums on the song. He coincidentally had also worked with Eddie Kramer, who, as I understand, did some work on those early Zeppelin recordings, so Chris had some cool insight. Naturally, doing a Zeppelin song, the drum sound had to be amazing and Chris's insight, as well as his great playing, sort of accidentally wound up being perfect. He didn't even know I was doing this track until I walked in that night, and we were the only two there! So by default he was the drummer.

I transferred all the electronic drums and bass that I had done in my studio, and we miked up the kit. We did a subwoofer-style setup on the kick drum. We then put a second kick in front of the main one and a mic in front of that as well. What we got was this sort of subsonic low end that just added this extra thump to the kick drum sound. It was perfect.

How did you record the guitar—mics and amps?

We recorded the SLO 100 through my Soldano 2 × 12 closed-back cab with two different mics: the Royer R-121 Ribbon and the RØDE NT-2. We discovered this combo about three years ago while recording my first record, *Rebirth*. The Royer is the only mic that lets me hear the amp the way it sounds in the room. There have been so many times where the amp sounded great in the room and flat in the control room. From there, we went to an API preamp, then a Motu HD192 to the computer.

What format did you record the song on?

We recorded digitally and mixed to an Otari two-track tape machine. I use Logic for all my programming. From there we transferred my programmed parts to Digital Performer,

Chapter 2 From the Horse's Mouth: Gunslinger

where we recorded the guitars and live drums. We did two different mixes, and Chris told me to pick which one I preferred. One was mixed to the analog tape machine, the other to the computer—all digital.

Give us a little background of the song and how you envisioned the guitar sounding?

This being a guitar instrumental performance, I wanted to have the guitar cover everything. The breakdown in the middle where John Bonham had this very long drum solo, I wanted the guitar to represent all those elements, rhythmic and textural. I did this pulsating low-end bed using a tremolo effect and did all this atmospheric stuff on top and built into the solo. It's one of my favorite parts of the track. Duplicating vocals has its challenges, though Robert Plant is so expressive and rhythmic that it translates quite well to guitar.

Neal Schon Has His I on U

Not many guitarists have such a rich musical history as Neal Schon. He made his musical debut with Santana as rhythm guitarist in the late '60s at age 16 and went on to cofound the band Journey with bandmate Gregg Rolie. What's wonderful about Neal is that he's always remained musically active with his side projects outside of the mega-hit-making machine Journey. Who could forget his great collaboration with Jan Hammer in the '80s? That's why I wasn't surprised to find his solo release on Favored Nations entitled *I on U* to be creative and refreshing. Neal, working alongside Russian keyboardist-sequencer Igor Len, put together 12 tracks showcasing Neal's classic rock tones with the modern drum programming flair of Igor. The haunting melodies of Neal's guitar-driven tracks flowing over the lush keyboard changes induce a sophisticated, cinematic feel throughout the album—but without forsaking his shredding, screaming leads and signature tone.

I had the pleasure of sitting down and speaking with Neal Schon about *I on U* and his new journey with Journey.

Were you influenced by anything in particular when you wrote the album? I know it's different from your Higher Octave releases. I like your tone much better on *I on U*.

I definitely wanted to give it a bit more of an edge. On the Higher Octave releases, I recorded what they wanted and dabbled in that area for a bit, and it was fun for a second. But I look at it like each solo project should all be different. I don't want to repeat myself on any one record; I'd rather go all over different genres.

***I on U* is a great album. I love the instrumental vibe—it just sings with great composing. I like how you combined your signature sound along with urban new grooves. Can you tell us a little about it?**

I worked with a keyboardist by the name of Igor Len. Working with him reminded me a lot of working with Jan Hammer. Igor is right up there with Jan and a very talented musician and composer. We just went at it every day and came up with the material. We sort of just winged it with Pro Tools, as opposed to going into the studio with a very structured schedule. I think I do my best when I'm not thinking about it too much; more off the cuff and from the heart, not the brain.

What's your recording setup on *I on U*?

It was mostly direct. I used a lot of Roland gear, the GP6 and plug-in amp simulators. It was all done on Pro Tools. I did a lot of programming on the GP6. When you do not have access to a large studio where you can set up a couple of great-sounding amps, the GP6 is a great alternative. I didn't have a working studio at the time, so we just used an empty room and set up shop and laid down the tracks. Then we sent it out to Gary Cirimelli at Amulet Music in Nashville.

The title track, "Revelation," on the new Journey album is a guitar instrumental. How did that come about?

I had the chord changes in my head and was working on creating a power ballad, a bit darker with classical-oriented changes like the old Journey song "Mother Father" from the album *Escape*. Producer Kevin Shirley encouraged me to put an instrumental on this record. I went home with a few ideas and played the chord structures down to a little digital recorder and laid down some guitar and drum loops. I really liked the way it came out and played it for Kevin, who loved it. Kevin then edited down the song a bit and had me cut it live for the record. We also added a longer intro and did some trippy reverse guitar on the outro.

The album was recorded at the Plant in Studio B in Sausalito, which has an old Neve Desk with a couple of 24-track analog Studer recording machines. We also used the new Pro Tools HD, which has some really impressive converter sounds. I was amazed by the fidelity and how much Pro Tools had improved. The old Pro Tools sounds used to leave me cold, because everything got squashed in the middle and it didn't have that giant spectrum of fidelity that you get out from using analog tape. You get low, low bottom end and nice highs and nice mids that sound like night and day from the old Pro Tools. We then had it engineered by John Neff and mixed by Kevin Shirley at Studio at the Palms, Las Vegas.

Being a real professional, Neal understands his craft and the making of a good-sounding record. For those of you who want to delve into Neal's solo side, I recommend picking up *I on U* from Favored Nations. Keeping with his classic Journey sound, "Revelation" is a true journey into his self-preservation of his craft.

Zakk Wylde: Wylde Child

It's hard to believe that it's been 20 years since Zakk Wylde replaced the late, great Randy Rhoads in Ozzy Osbourne's band. Even though there were a couple of guitarists before him, Zakk is truly the only guitarist who did the gig justice. The Wylde Irish boy from New Jersey really showed the world he could take the guitar farther than any of his predecessors, and in the past two decades with Ozzy, as well as in his own solo projects, he has emerged as a major influence to metal guitarists everywhere.

Thinking back to the early '80s, I remember when Randy Rhoads played guitar for Ozzy and how in awe we all were of Randy's techniques on those two groundbreaking records, *Diary of a Madman* and *Blizzard of Ozz*. When Zakk came along, everyone was wondering how anyone would be able to follow in Randy's footsteps, but Zakk proved himself to be worthy of the task and then some. In 1992, when I saw Zakk at the Coconut Teaser in LA with his southern rock band, Pride and Glory, I was able to see what an amazing showman he was and hear his great vocal talents as well. I later picked up a Randy Coven album with the song "I Wish" on it, and there was Zakk singing his heart out, sounding very much like Gregg Allman. Later, in the '90s, he formed the heavier-than-thou band Black Label Society. He has released eight albums with them, most recently *Shot to Hell*.

I had the pleasure of rapping with Zakk on the phone about everything from his three kids to recording *Shot to Hell* and beyond.

Where was *Shot to Hell* recorded?

We used Ameraycan Studios in North Hollywood.

What is your typical guitar and amp setup?

For guitars, I'll bring the Les Paul and the Rock Replica Randy Rhoads polka dot V guitar made by GMW Guitar Works that I like to use on solos. I will also use a 12-string and 6-string acoustic—I bring the whole arsenal.

I like to go through different amps to see what works, but I'll usually use just one. I'll bring the Marshall JMP, JCM800, and JCM2000, but usually use the 800. I will also bring a Roland JC-120 Jazz Chorus. You bring all your crayons with you; it's not like you're going to use all 64 of them, but if you need them, they're there.

Any pedals you can't live without?

I have a milk crate full of all sorts of pedals. I always bring my pedal board that I use live. The Dunlop Chorus pedal, the MXR ZW-44 Wylde Overdrive Pedal, the Van Halen MXR Phase 90, the Dunlop Uni-Vibe, and the Dunlop Wah pedal. Whether it's for Ozzy or Black Label Society, they all work great for me.

What are your main axes?

I leave the "Holy Grail"—my original 1981 custom Les Paul—at home now. I use the Gibson Signature Bullseye Flying V with EMG pickups and my Custom Les Paul.

Did you record the album analog or digital?

It's recorded all analog. We didn't rehearse; we just went into the studio and wrote the record—that's where all the magic happens. We'll then dump it into Pro Tools if we need to shorten it or copy and paste. We record the whole album in one shot, and then dump it down digitally. Back in the day, when we recorded everything on analog, if you had to edit something you had to cut tape, and if you made a mistake you were screwed.

What about mics?

I like the Shure SM57.

How did you come up with the cover of the nuns playing pool and hanging with the devils inside the booklet? And that close-up of you in full devil makeup?

A buddy of mine owns a bar in Santa Clarita, and the people at the photo shoot were like someone's grandmother or grandfather. They were just hanging out having a great time posing for these pictures, and we were all drinking all day and laughing hysterically at these characters. They were great people to work with, and we had a lot of fun doing it. The next day, I woke up on the sofa with my makeup still on—the horns still stuck to my forehead—and when my little boy saw me he started touching the horns on my head and screaming, "I want my daddy back!" I probably ruined him for life. That will win me the Father of the Year award in *Good Housekeeping*!

Martin Winch: State of "Kashmir"

The late Martin Winch is one of those great discoveries whose music has a way of warming the heart. With his nylon guitar playing, one could not help but feel inspired to participate in the experience. His appealing style of ambient, acoustic, and electric guitar melodies—reminiscent of Larry Carlton's tone and feel—really drew you in, to say the least. When I stumbled upon this guitarist from New Zealand, I thought he would be a wonderful addition to the *Guitar Masters* compilation series.

A veteran of the music business for more than 35 years, Winch released five solo albums on his own, and he taught all styles of guitar. In his home recording studio, he produced and composed music for commercials, documentaries, and AV productions. One of these was the popular New Zealand Toyota commercial "Welcome to Our World," which showcased his various styles, ranging from country to raunchy rock, from folk to jazz.

He worked in several New Zealand groups, including Dr. Tree (Jazz Album of the Year, 1976), Mike Harvey's Salty Dogg, and later the famous 1860 Band in Wellington. He also appeared at two Montreux Jazz Festivals with the Roger Fox Big Band and was honored with the Guitarist of the Year award in Auckland, New Zealand, in 1999. Winch was also a part of the Club 21 resident band Billboard in the mid-1980s.

Before his untimely passing, I spoke with Winch about his wonderful acoustic rendition of the Zeppelin tune "Kashmir" and got the lowdown on his recording techniques.

What was your setup for recording "Kashmir"?

My initial demo of "Kashmir" was an electric version more like the original, but I decided I hadn't changed it enough to warrant anyone being interested in it. So I just started programming Middle Eastern drum samples to give it a more exotic flavor. I decided to try it with acoustic guitars rather than electric, and it seemed to work. The solo sections, although they don't sound like it, are still based on the chords that Led Zep used. I used MIDI from an old Atari computer program for all of the other instruments. It will die on me one day, but until then I will continue to use it. The main sound modules I use are a

Roland 1080 fitted with soundcards for bass and drums, and a Yamaha Motif rack. My studio is pretty small, so there is not enough room for drum kits and big amps.

Do you have your own recording studio?

I used my own home studio to record everything, with a selection of mics by AKG, CAD, and Studio Projects (all condenser mics). My mic preamp is locally made by DJR, featuring Neve-style EQ options. I generally record in stereo with two mics on the guitar quite close, to avoid any fan or other noise from the PC.

How did you record your guitar tracks?

On the recording of "Kashmir" I used four acoustic guitars: a Seagull Grand Artist (parlor-style guitar) for all the rhythm chord parts; a Matsuoka nylon guitar for the first ad lib section; and a Martin D-35 for the second ad lib section. Then I played the slide melody on a 1980 Epiphone semiacoustic with the action raised up high using a large Allen key under the strings! There is also a lick in there recorded on a Hofner six-string banjo.

What was your recording format?

My recording equipment is all PC-based, and I use Cubase to record with. I have lots of software for effects and mixing. I have Yamaha NS10s and a pair of Yorkville ported monitors for near-field mixing, and some large RCF speakers for the big sound. I am completely self-taught, both on the guitar and as a sound engineer, and have spent most of my life doing one or the other.

What projects are you working on?

I am currently planning an album of easy-on-the-ear tunes, with lots of strings and me playing mostly nylon guitar. I have, in the past, had some success with this type of album in New Zealand and Australia, but unfortunately we weren't able to get a release in the U.S.

Larry Van Fleet: Getting the Led Out

When putting together the *Guitar Masters* series, I discovered a terrific unknown guitarist from the Midwest by the name of Larry Van Fleet. He had a song called "Hummingbird Rag," which showcased an incredible acoustic fingerstyle. As it turns out, he had done a fair share of gigging, as well as studying Master Classes with Miguel Rubio and Charlie Byrd (which explained his flawless approach to guitar playing). Unfortunately, the lineup was already filled for *Guitar Masters*, but I knew he would be perfect for another CD I was producing, called *Get the Led Out! A Led Zeppelin Salute*. He agreed to do a song for the compilation and delved into the project immediately, resulting in an amazing instrumental version of the song "D'yer Maker."

What was your recording setup for "D'yer Maker"?

I recorded my interpretation of Led Zeppelin's "D'yer Maker" on a '79 Gibson ES-347TD. All three-guitar tracks, rhythm, slide, and lead went through a Line 6 PODXT via

USB to a Carillon AC-1 PC. The PODXT is equipped with the Effects pack, the Bass pack, and the FBV Shortboard pedal controller. I recorded the bass track using a Peavey Millennium bass also through the PODXT.

What's your studio like?

Karaya6 Studio is a small den in my house in Omaha, Nebraska. The room is 9 feet by 11 feet, carpeted, with bookshelves and no acoustic treatment. "D'yer Maker" was recorded entirely within this studio using the PODXT into the Carillon AC-1. I mixed the tracks on a pair of Alesis M1 active monitors and A-B'd the mixes with my car stereo and an old component system at home. Since this recording was digitally "in the box," I had the advantage of working late at night or during the day without household and neighborhood noises destroying takes. I recorded without headphones, referencing the tracks through the M1s. Later, I checked the tracks and mix with a set of Sony MDR7506 headphones. I used drum loops from Siggi Baldursson's "Drum Sugar" (Sony ACID Loops). A particular intro loop caught my ear, and the rest of the groove had the feel that I was looking for.

How did you record the guitars?

The PODXT lets me dial in every parameter of a particular sound and in the end gives a pretty convincing impression of a miked amp. I have several user-defined presets that I tweak and save, which generally helps me to overcome my audio engineering limitations and proceed with the music. For this track, I modified the presets for each of the three guitar sounds. I had intended to use a Hamer, but it was in need of adjustment at the time of the recording, so the Gibson got the call. In the end, I was pleased with the warm, attractive tone it imparted to the mix.

How did you plan the sound?

I was attracted to the song "D'yer Maker" by the slightly reggae vibe and the over-the-top delivery by Zep. Basically, the song is a ballad, and they sing and play it as an angst-ridden parody. I liked the tongue-in-cheek approach and the groove. Since I couldn't get lost in the arrangement, and being a firm believer in the happy accident, I laid down the drum loops, bass, and rhythm guitar and got my slide out.

The 347 is unadjusted and in standard tuning for the slide track. I used a slap-back echo with flange and threw caution to the wind. The one plan that I did follow was to have the slide guitar "reply" to the lead in the B section. I wanted to use the volume pedal on the lead guitar, but once I played with adjusting the auto-swell, I was hooked on the way it made me phrase the lines and I just let it flow.

What's on the horizon?

Recent projects from late 2007 and early 2008 included two pieces recorded for Bohemian Productions: a Jeff Beck tribute, for which I interpreted "Water Down the Drain" from the '69 release *Beckola*, and a Jimi Hendrix tribute where I caught up with "You Got Me Floatin'" from the '67 *Axis: Bold as Love*. I make ongoing contributions to [film music libraries] Spider Cues, Editor's Choice, and DSM Producers of New York and was recently featured in two independent films by D. Sawatski, *The Grove* and *Running*.

A Gibson 347 was a terrific choice for the song; I never would've guessed that he used a semihollow body on the track. It amazes me, an old analog dog, that an artist like Larry can make a simple den into a functioning recording environment with merely a computer and software. It's just a sign of how far we've come; musicians can now create and record their ideas and tracks on such a full palette of options.

Studio Journey with Larry Carlton

As Larry Carlton has shown throughout his multifaceted career as a first-class session guitarist and a successful recording artist, the Gibson ES-335 guitar is his voice. From playing with such stars as Herb Alpert, Quincy Jones, Michael Jackson, John Lennon, and Jerry Garcia to joining the Crusaders, where his guitar playing really came into his own style, Larry showed his prolific styles.

In the 1970s, he built his own home studio, which he named Room 335. He went on to produce, co-write (with Michel Columbier), and arrange the acclaimed movie soundtrack for *Against All Odds*. *Rolling Stone* magazine listed Carlton's tasty ascent on Steely Dan's "Kid Charlemagne" as one of the three best guitar licks in rock music. By the early 1980s, Carlton had picked up four Grammy nominations along the way. In 1981, he won a Grammy for his collaboration with Mike Post for the theme to *Hill Street Blues*.

I had the pleasure of sitting down with Mr. 335 one hot summer afternoon in New York's West Side at his hotel lobby. He was as modest as he was gracious and talented. As many of you know, Larry had a world-class recording studio back in the '70s and '80s in LA. We discussed everything from his new rerecorded hits CD released on his new label, 335 Records, to being a part of Fourplay to his beginnings with Joe Sample in the Crusaders.

Who will you be playing with tonight at the Blue Note?

One of the world's greatest drummers, Billy Kilson, who just happens to be on a two-week vacation and only lives 20 miles outside of the city. We're having a ball. He and I have not played together in five years. And my son Travis on bass … killing … killing! He just turned 26 in April. He's been touring with me for four years, out with Robben Ford as well. When I'm not out, Robben swoops him up. He's going to do another album for Robben in January. He's got the gift. I'm so proud! No keys, it's a trio. I started doing a trio last year to do something different. And it's really fun. It's so open, I have to use my harmony now a lot more and a lot of chord stuff also. I'm on a three-week tour in the U.S., and then I go to the Tokyo Jazz Festival next week with Fourplay. Everyone is busy; it's good.

Tell me about your new greatest hits CD.

We rerecorded everything. I took songs from certain periods of my career. We did "Room 335" from 1979 and "Smiles and Smiles to Go." On 90 percent of the tunes, I tried to make them sound just like the originals when they first came out. So you might put "Smiles and Smiles" on from the rerecorded hits version and say, "Oh, I know that," but obviously all of the solos are different and other little sections are different. So it's really fun to do a tease and then new versions of the tunes. It was a cool project.

What players did you use for this recording?

Travis on bass. Jeff Babko, one of LA's best keyboardists. We call him wonder child because he is so gifted and he's only 36 years old. And on drums, Vinnie Calaiuta. Strong band. I still had all of the old charts, so I said to them, "You've heard them on the radio, so now let's redo them."

Did you record it in your own studio?

No, we recorded it all at Capitol Recording in the B room with Csaba Petocz engineering it. I built my own studio, and it's basically a production room. I have a 200-year-old two-and-a-half-story log cabin that we converted on my property into my Pro Tools room. We actually added a vocal booth and a storage area room, where I can put all of my amps and let them breathe. So I can choose any of my amps when I record.

So no more analog gear. You had quite a studio back in the day. Do you do everything in the box?

Yeah, I did have a big studio back then. But today 99 percent of the time I mostly use it as a preproduction studio. Because usually I get all of my performances live in the studio, so I don't have to replace any guitars. So I only use it as preproduction recording when I'm writing the songs. And then I'll just go direct into the computer and pick a sound from Amp Farm or just use the direct sound. I just want the guys to know what the parts and the feel are supposed to sound like. And then we'll go back and record it with the whole band in another studio. To me, who hears the difference between analog and digital? The listener just hears the music, unless it is offensive. They either like the song or get a feeling from the song, or they don't. I'm really at that point where it is all about the music, as well as the quality.

For the final mix do you go somewhere else?

Yes, Csaba Petocz. For the last three to four years, Csaba has been such a world-class engineer that I just turn that all over to him. Now with Fourplay we all just camp out for two weeks in the studio and hand over the final mixes to the engineer. With the Internet the engineer sends us mixes to approve. I got a couple of emails from old friends who are getting ready to do new recordings and asked me to solo on them, and I said, "Just send me the files via the Internet, and I'll play on it." It's great—I don't have to leave the house.

Do you have any favorite mics you use when you are recording?

I knew you were going to go to the technical thing, so I have to be honest. Starting eight or nine years ago, I honestly relinquished that all to the engineer. I'm a guitarist. I don't stay up on the hippest, hottest condenser mics. I just hire the best guys I know, and whatever mic they decide sounds the best on my amp, I usually agree. Put it this way: In '02 I recorded four sides with a smooth jazz producer in LA that Warner suggested. So I went in, and all I took was my guitar. He had an old blackface Fender amp sitting around and put a 251 mic in front of it, and I cut the four tunes. It didn't matter what amp was there—it sounds like me, and we got two number-one radio hits off of it.

I use to labor, placing the mic half an inch off of the cone center, et cetera. But now I've really come to a different perspective. For example, I recorded "Firewire," which was in '04, and Csaba produced it. He had a sound in mind for my guitar for the tunes. We went into Capitol Recording, and it was interesting. The drums, bass, and guitar were set up in the big room, but my amp was in a smaller room, where he left the door to the smaller room cracked so there would be a very subtle amount of leakage from the amp onto the drum mics. Csaba really had a vision on how he wanted to present me. I even let him set my Dumble amp. I would just play, and he would start twisting knobs and then go back in the control room. He designed my sound for that album.

Going back to your classic recordings of "Room 335" and *Strikes Twice*, was your approach to recording different?

Back then, I was still using my Mesa Boogie. It didn't have a name like Mark I or II; it was just one of the first made. I was very anal back then about sound, because I was a young engineer but an experienced guitar player-arranger. So I had to go through the process. I spent hours on the kick drum, but when a big boy engineer would come in, he would just place it in a matter of minutes. So I would try an 87 back 3 feet and a 57 on the cone but then had to move the 57 around. So I went through all of that.

You've been playing a Dumble amp for long time now. How do they differ from the old Mesa Boogies?

I've been playing Dumble for almost 25 years. There is no comparison to sound and approach to Mesas. I stopped using the Boogies around 1982. I had two, the original two I had purchased, and over the years the capacitors had dried up and had to be rebuilt. Randy Smith over at Boogie was wonderful to me. He went through all of my specs on my amp and built me another one, trying to duplicate the originals, but they didn't quite sound as good as the originals. So when I discovered the Dumble, my tone went way up. The quality of the sound went way up, and I kind of noticed over the years the sound of Boogie seemed very processed. And I didn't relate to that. So I have two Dumbles, one for stage and one for backup. The head is separate, and the speaker cabinet, which Dumble designed, was made to go with the head. I use a 1 × 12 speaker cabinet with my head.

So Gibson designed your own signature series guitar?

Yeah, how flattering is that? I know they're back ordered. My '69 that I've played for years is subtly different in many ways than a stock 335. I just got lucky in 1969 when I picked my 335 at a music store; out of the three or four they had, I picked the best-sounding one. And sure enough, that sucker is warm, not dark. Sings like an angel, but not bright. The only thing I did is replace the trapeze for a stop tailpiece. No pickup changes or anything. I got lucky, so we just tried to re-create that warmth.

Will you be playing tracks from your hits CD tonight at the Blue Note?

I'm not, only because I'm playing in a trio setting, and most of those songs are production songs. Without the background pads, you're not going to want to hear me play certain songs. I can't even play "Sleepwalk." So actually, on this tour we have been playing six new originals I've written that the audience has never heard. Though we still do "Smiles and Smiles to Go," and we encore with "Josie." I would say the new material is a little more jazz—harmonically and feel wise—but it still opens up so I can do whatever it is I want to do for a solo. One of the tunes is a real funky kind of tune that actually Fourplay cut on their new album, because they liked it so much. Then a couple of the others are more fusion oriented, with darker sounds and harmonies.

Looking back at your career, how much did the Crusaders influence you as a player?

It was in 1971 when I started recording with them, and I did 13 albums with them over the next six and a half years. In '71 I was 23 years old and in my formative years. The first week on recording with the Crusaders they did a cover version of Carole King's "So Far Away." And I was using the volume pedal, making crying little notes. It was really new back then; nobody was doing that. And they told me after the recording that, after they heard the crying guitar sounds, the producer and the engineer in the booth said to each other, "What the hell was that?" They hadn't heard anything like that or at least the way I did it. So yeah, we kind of created a new sound early in the '70s.

Today I still approach my music in a similar way to how the Crusaders approached theirs. You get a great little hook; you get an idea about the production line. Maybe you have a bass line for letter A or maybe you don't. You find it in the studio, if you didn't get it in the preproduction. Then in the studio you go for the performance. Very seldom—I mean *very* seldom—will I overdub anything at home. The magic happens in the studio for performance.

Performing live with the Crusaders in those days, Joe Sample would like to break the band down. After the head happened and somebody else's solo happened, Joe would bring us way down dynamically, so he could start his thing and could get into his solo section. And I do that on almost every song today. That's where the freedom comes; it gets soft, and there is an open palette. You can go left, right, and straight, up, down, wherever you want to go. Then the moments of coolness can happen. And I still do it that way.

Prior to the Crusaders, I was doing session work and had my own trios and quartets playing around Los Angeles. Joe heard me on a session, and that's how I got to join the band. We were all very busy, and with the success the Crusaders had, they could be very choosy about what shows they'd play live. So we would only go out on weekends or a small tour of Japan. In North Hollywood, originally in the 1970s through the '80s, there was a local club called Donte's, and that's where I would end up playing with Joe Sample. It seemed like there were two camps: the camp that would play Donte's and the camp that would play the Baked Potato. I chose Donte's because I was invited to play there once. I was comfortable there, and we sold out every show. It was Joe Sample, Pops Popwell, Jeff Porcaro, Greg Mathieson, and I. But Dave Grusin, Tom Scott, and all of these other guys would be playing the Baked Potato. Eventually it all intertwined, and you would play wherever you wanted.

How do you feel about today's commercial jazz market and your role in Fourplay?

I think when the smooth jazz format started, it was a watered-down version of what had preceded it. Like Herbie [Hancock] and the Headhunters and David Sanborn—guys who were really playing but happened to catch the public anyway. My impression of this commercial jazz market, especially when it started, was they were just trying to imitate and format it so they could just get more listeners. I think it really did water down the quality. A lot of the artists you'd hear in the smooth jazz market had no voice; it could be any one of nine sax players. Though successful, I don't think it was artistically very fulfilling. And I don't think it is the ground for presenting the cream of the crop, which the industry should be presenting, in my opinion. The artists that deserve to be heard, not guys that just play okay and produce nice little ditties.

I've been with Fourplay for 12 years now, and when Fourplay first started they had such huge success with no notion to make a hit record, but they sounded different from everything else that was going on. We still don't say, "We need to get on the radio," with this album. But you can't stop Bob James from being a creative genius. He is just full of music. For example, we had recorded for about five days, and Bob had this idea, which he had not spoken to us about, on doing a Bach piece, but the way Fourplay would do it. So he just charted it out and put some chord symbols over certain places, and we just started playing Bach. So that night Bob took what we had done back to his room and finessed it as an arranger. He came in the next day, and we had this original piece inspired by Bach.

You also have your own record label?

Yes, I started 335 Records with my manager, Robert Williams. The first thing I was fortunate enough to release was the Larry Carlton with special guest Robben Ford *Live in Tokyo*. I also released the rerecorded hits albums as well. I have a female jazz singer, Laurie Wheeler—she's going to sit in this week with me at the Blue Note. Laurie is really special. We went in the studio with her, Jeff Babko, Toss Panos, and myself and released it on my label. We hired an indie jazz radio promoter and had 169 radio stations playing Laurie's record.

The label is fun. I can record anything I like at any time. I have a couple things in the can. Robben and I did an acoustic live album in Paris and also a DVD. At some point in the future it will come out. So yeah, it is good! We don't have physical distribution now. We have people calling us all of the time. But we are moving very slowly, because we don't want to fall back into the old-school record company thing. It's not working! There's a better way to do it nowadays. And we're in the process with the Internet, advertising, live performances, but we're very close to making a distribution deal for Europe and Japan.

For the past 15 years, Mr. 335 has been living a tranquil life with his wife on their small farm just outside of Nashville, Tennessee. He has four horses and four dogs and does a lot of trout fishing on his days off. In 2009, Larry picked up two more Grammy nominations, bringing his career total to 18 nominations with three Grammy wins. Larry's *Greatest Hits Rerecorded, Volume 1*, released on 335 Records, was nominated for Best Pop Instrumental Album, and Fourplay's "Fortune Teller," on the *Energy* album, was nominated for Best Pop Instrumental Performance. Even in his 60s, Larry is still a driving force of inspiration for guitar players and the recording industry. It's no wonder that his warm personality and great vibe seem to transcend through his remarkable guitar tone from his beloved 335!

Ted Nugent: Guitar Tone in the Mix

Let's start with a comment from Nugent:

"Though there are many moments of tonal splendor throughout Love Grenade where my 59 Les Pauls join the fray, plus the occasional throttling on those very special hollow-body PRS masterpieces as well, it is the combination of Peavey 6505s and some old pre-CBS Fender Twin amps that ultimately make the sound so wonderful. Regarding my choice to change up guitars and amps off and on during my adventurous musical career, it is a direct result of being a music fan first and foremost, and in my inexhaustible quest for the ultimate guitar tone."

So obviously, you can take various steps during recording, constantly adjusting your source, until you find the tone that works for a particular song. This is a very important point, because how many of us sit in a music store and get great tone out of a particular device or effect pedal, but find that once we bring it back to the studio, it absolutely doesn't work in the mix? Ironically, this can work in reverse, where you play an effect pedal and think to yourself, "Where in the world would I ever use it?" Of course, two days later when you're back in the studio, you try that particular sound for a quirky idea and voilà—it's perfect for the song.

However, when you record your guitar tones, the real trick is the treatment in the mix to make a statement. Of course, this all depends on the style of music; for example, guitar instrumental music will be treated much differently than pop rock. But regardless, there are certain easy measures to keep that guitar distinct. One is a good old-fashioned EQ process. Since I own a studio, I'm a bit spoiled by having a Trident desk at my fingertips with 32 channels of EQ. But there are plenty of EQ plug-ins today that will do the trick.

The important thing to remember is not to overdo it. You want a little boost in the mids, but not too much that the guitar is too brittle. The best way is to really experiment and see how the particular guitar sits in track. Listen to the mix on as many different speakers as possible and see the common ground. There are many factors involved, from the type of music to the type of guitar used, so there really isn't any norm to follow. I found using a parametric EQ rack is very useful in terms of being able to really pinpoint the frequency you would like to boost. Orban made a number of broadcast ones that you can find for a couple hundred dollars on eBay. There is a Pultec plug-in that also works well.

Another way to really control guitar is the use of a limiter or compressor. It works like a charm and really helps keep the guitar in the mix. In fact, compressors give guitars presence, and they control the various dynamics, particularly on bass and crunchy rhythm guitar. I found using the mic pre/compressor Universal Audio LA-610 specifically useful. One of the wonderful things about the unit is the onboard EQ—very subtle but great on acoustic guitar, lead guitar, and even bass.

For those of you who are not familiar with LA-610, it is a channel strip format based on the legendary console modules developed by Bill Putnam back in the 1960s. It combines the 610 Mic-Pre/EQ/DI sections and a T4 Opto-compressor. Because of its tube circuitry, it creates a very musical character and warmth. But one of my absolute favorite compressors is the Urei LA-4, which absolutely loves all guitars. The great thing about the LA-4 is that it is very transparent, capturing your tone and controlling the level in the mix. Extremely easy to use, I would recommend it highly, even if it were the only compressor you ever bought.

Whether you are recording on hard disk or you are an old analog dawg like me, there are many factors involved when making the guitar track take shape in the mix. The best way to approach it is to make sure you can hear every instrument in the mix along with the guitar. If the guitar is the lead instrument, then treat it like you would lead vocals, as you can clearly hear in Satriani mixes. If your guitar is a rhythm instrument like in many of the Nug man's songs, make sure you have sonic room for other instruments, including the vocals. Sonically, one of the most interesting portraits is Eric Johnson's use of various guitar tones via real amps to achieve a wonderful musical canvas. He uses different guitars and amps to get a clean sound, as opposed to his overdriven sound. This makes the most sense; some cats get so attached to a certain guitar or amp that they lock themselves out for change. For example, if you want a 12-string sound, don't just plug in a chorus pedal—use a real 12-string.

But the most interesting conclusion is that the best achievements are the combination of digital technology and analog, the best of both worlds. I'll leave you with the immensely charismatic message that Ted passed on to me.

"Ah yes, the sweet smoky BBQ grease drip of the mighty Gibson Byrdland in the hands of a pure, primal-scream aboriginal dogman fresh from a steaming gut pile campfire somewhere way back in the Spirit Wild hinterland that we all love so dearly. Such romance! It is indeed the unleashing of numerous Byrdlands from my glowing arsenal of assault guitars that were not turned over to the evil government when they attempted to ban them years ago. It is insanely fun and the guitar tone is merely the manifestation of our united love."

Gary Hoey: Stratocaster Burn

Gary Hoey may not be a household name, but he has enjoyed a well-respected guitar career and is a verified guitar god. Gary has a collection of 16 albums and five top-20 Billboard hits, and he is listed in the top 100 greatest guitar players of all time. A lot of us remember his 1993 breakthrough remake of "Hocus Pocus" on Warner Bros. Records, which landed him a top-five position on the Billboard charts. The Boston-raised guitarist followed up with the soundtrack to the surf saga *Endless Summer II*. And who can forget his popular *Ho! Ho! Hoey Christmas* releases? Gary has played with the best of them: Brian May (Queen), Ted Nugent, Foreigner, Joe Satriani, the Doobie Brothers, Kenny Wayne Shepherd, Eric Johnson, Steve Vai, Peter Frampton, Rick Derringer, and Deep Purple.

So of course, Gary was a top choice when I was putting together the compilation, *Guitar Masters, Volume 3 & 4: Les Paul Dedication*. I chose him for the classic Jeff Beck remake of "El Becko," and he performed flawlessly. His phrasing of the melody and solo tradeoffs with me was a marriage made in shred heaven! Gary recently released his 16th album, titled *Utopia*, and he explains how he got his ripping sound in the studio, giving us some useful tricks and tips of the trade.

Congratulations on your latest release, *Utopia*. What was your typical setup during recording: guitar, amp, pedals, et cetera? Were there any particular artists or songs at the time that influenced you?

I play Fender Strats. One of my two main guitars for recording is my Blue Strat with the lefty neck. It has a great sound for heavier songs ("Walk Away," "Reminds Me of You"). It has two humbuckers. Seymour Duncan JB in the bridge and a '59 in the neck and an ebony fretboard and a quilted maple top. I had a lefty neck put in because I thought it looked cool like Hendrix, but I found out the bass strings are longer on a lefty, so you get this fat tone. I string with GHS, 10 through 50. It's a 10 set with bigger bass strings I tune to E flat. My other main guitar is my FLAG Strat, which I used on many solos and bluesy tracks ("Something's Going On," "Simplify"). Master builder Jon Cruz Fender Custom Shop built it. It has a mini Seymour JB humbucker in the bridge and Texas specials. It's a 1960 relic.

How did the process go? Were the guitar parts written in the studio or already laid out? Or did you go to the studio and improvise on solos?

I used several amps on *Utopia*. The main amp was the EVH 5150III. It's an amazing three-channel amp. Many people don't know how amazing it is. (Don't tell anyone.) I also used the Peavey Triple XXX, DIEZEL, and a Marshall. For some of the heavier tones, like "Walk Away," I laid eight rhythm tracks. One sound would be bassier, and one more midrange—and when you combine them, it's huge. You have to play super tight and mix the levels carefully, just sneaking in a tone.

What microphones were used to record the guitar parts? Did you record in a studio or in a home studio? Take us through a little bit of the recording process and the gear.

I used a few pedals. My signature pedal, Skull Crusher by HomeBrew Electronics, has a gain boost with a fat compression and not a lot of crunch. I also used the Power Screamer by HBE, the Rocktron Metal Planet, and the Austin Distortion. Dunlop Cry Baby and Rocktron Cyborg Delay in the loop of the amp.

My process for this album was to turn the demos into a record. So I mapped out all the songs in Pro Tools at my home studio. All with the drum loops in a grid. I miked my amps so if I played a good solo, the tone would be usable. I improvised all the solos but did a few comps. I would play several takes and then comp the best parts to make a good solo. Pretty standard these days.

I recorded the guitars with one Shure SM57. The best guitar mic, hands down. I placed it slightly off center and close to the grill cloth. I don't use far ambient mics. I think it's better to add reverb later, if you want it. I always mix the rhythm guitars bone dry and in your face. And never record with any delay or reverb. Once you add it, you're stuck with it. I ran it through a chain of Groove Tubes Mic Pre and EQ. Very little compression.

What first attracted you to being a guitar instrumentalist? How did you accomplish your vision of getting your guitar tone recorded?

The first attraction I had to instrumental guitar was through Jeff Beck and Al Di Meola. So I would study *Blow by Blow* by Jeff and *Elegant Gypsy* by Al Di Meola. Then Joe

Satriani, Steve Vai, and Eric Johnson showed that you could make it commercially viable. When I signed to Warner Bros. Records in 1992, we released *Heavy Bones* (now out of print, available on eBay only), and when the band got crushed by Nirvana, I went instrumental. I worked with Richie Zito on *Heavy Bones*. Richie had produced many great albums, including some by Cheap Trick and the Cult. What he taught me was to have many amps and guitars, because changing an amp for different tempos and keys can make all the difference.

Do you have a favorite can't-live-without guitar processor/effects that you used on your scores?

Rocktron Prophesy II Pre-Amp and the Fender Cyber-Twin SE. Great amps.

What projects are you working on currently?

I've been honing my producer skills for years. So I'm producing and writing with Lita Ford. Just finished producing the band Switchblade Glory, with Andy Johns mixing. Lukas Rossi is the singer; he won on the TV show *Rock Star Supernova*. Amazing singer. Also produced a young female named Madison Rose. I recorded a new Christmas CD for Fall 2011. I love to work with other artists and bring my knowledge. I've been on both sides of the glass, so I know what they are going through.

Anything you'd like to add, any guitar recording tips or advice?

My advice is to try different things. You can fall into the best things by goofing around. Happy accidents, I call them. I worked for three months with Roy Thomas Baker (who produced Queen, the Cars, Journey, et cetera), and he showed me it's important to try anything, push the envelope. And bend down and listen to what's coming out of the speaker. Many guitar players get their tone and don't bend to hear what's coming out. Moving the mic one inch can make it great. Also, I use the playlist feature on Pro Tools, do a bunch of takes, and later go through and comp the best. When I produce singers, I let them sing all the way through to get a performance. I don't stop them every time they mess up. Keep the flow. Most importantly, have fun and do what you love. Good luck!

Leslie West: Brown Tone

During producing and recording Randy Coven's release "Nu School," I had the amusement of working with guest guitarist Leslie West. For those of you who are not familiar with this guitar icon, West started his musical career with the '60s band the Vagrants. Felix Pappalardi, who was also producing the famed Disraeli Gears with Cream at the time, produced the recordings. In 1969, West and Pappalardi formed the pioneering band Mountain. A little-known fact for you Who fans is that West and keyboardist Al Kooper recorded with the Brit band during the March 1971 *Who's Next* New York sessions. Tracks include a cover of "Baby Don't You Do It" and early versions of "Love Ain't for Keepin'" and the Who's signature track, "Won't Be Fooled Again." Though the tracks were not originally included on the album, they appear as bonus tracks on reissues of *Who's Next*.

During the session, I was faced with many choices and options for recording the guitars accurately, in which microphones became the paramount ingredient. Mics are the true translation of guitar tones to recording and should be as accurate as possible. Every guitarist wants to record the sound he hears in the room through the amp. The question becomes, how? Like everything else in life, there are thousands of interpretations of why certain mics are better than others.

According to West:

> *"I used my custom Dean guitar through a Marshall JCM800 with a Robert Kelley modified Ibanez Tube Screamer. We near-miked the cabinet with a Beyer M 160 and five feet back miked it using a Neumann TLM 149. I want to feel the bottom boom of the cabinet, so we left the iso booth door open where the cabinet was and let it ring through the control room."*

I always like speaking to guitarists about how they get their tone and capture it onto a recording. Some are really basic, such as placing an SM57 in front of an amp, turning it to 11, and pressing the red button, while others painstakingly take hours to figure out the mechanics of where the sound projects best for mic placement. Following are some tips and tricks to help you get your tone recorded—and hopefully not drive yourself crazy trying numerous options.

Beyerdynamics M 160

The M 160 has to be one of my favorite guitar mics. A very simple design, but extremely effective for recording guitars. I've used it to record all types of guitar amps, open backs, closed backs, 1 × 12 combos to Marshall half-stacks, and the result is always the same—fantastic! During the Leslie West session, I used it to close-mike a Legacy cabinet, placing it halfway between the cone and the outer edge of the speaker. The mic's characteristics are very clean sounding, with a nice punch to the upper midfrequencies. Because it is a ribbon mic, it really captures the nuances of the guitar and amp. It's hard to believe that the company states that its manufacturing process for the M 160 has remained fundamentally unchanged since introducing the model in 1957. Ironically, it was originally developed as an alternative to the then-expensive condenser microphone. Nowadays, it seems that ribbon microphones have made a huge comeback and have become well known for their accurate reproduction.

Neumann TLM 49

The TLM 49 is a solid-state cardioid microphone with warm characteristics. I've used these mics on everything from guitar cabinets, sax, vocals, and even piano (in stereo pair). I usually use it in conjunction with another mic when recording guitar cabinets. For instance, I'll near-mike a Marshall cabinet with an M 160 and place the TLM 49 about five feet back. I did this on the Leslie West recordings, which did a nice job capturing the fat tone of the 4 × 12 cabinet. You get a nice clear image with M 160 and a thicker cabinet sound of the room with the TLM 49. I blend these two signals together during the mix, placing the M 160 signal a bit higher, while fading just enough of the TLM 49 to create a thicker depth of the guitar. Because the TLM 49 is a large-diaphragm microphone, I feel it captures a fuller, warmer sound of the guitar cabinets, creating a realistic recording of the sound you hear in the room.

Sennheiser MD 421

The 421, put simply, is an SM57 on steroids. It's probably one of the most diverse mics ever made. Most commonly used for miking toms, it has so much more potential than it's given credit for. For example, in the '60s, the Who and Bob Dylan used 421s as vocal mics, and later in the '70s, Eddie Van Halen used them for miking his guitar cabinets. In fact, the 421 shines in broadcasting applications, such as radio announcing, featuring the five-position bass control, which enhances its all-around qualities. I've used it for all of the purposes just mentioned, plus a plethora of other things, such as miking bass cabinets or horn sections.

A lot of engineers and producers use it in conjunction with an SM57 and a ribbon microphone to blend in and enhance certain frequencies of the guitar. I actually like using it with an SM57 as well, because it actually boosts the lower midfrequency, while the 57 records the higher frequencies of the guitar tones, creating complementary tones between the two. The wonderful advantage of the 421 is that it handles very high SPLs (*sound pressure levels*). Being a large-diaphragm dynamic microphone that came out originally in the early '60s, the 421 has been on almost every classic rock recording in some way or another. It was born to be a rock guitar mic.

AKG D 112/EV RE-20

Recording direct and miked signals is a great recipe for a huge bass sound in the mix. I use this method in many bass recordings, with the Radial J48 Direct Box as a buffer to split the signal. I plug the amp into the Radial's thru jack and plug the bass into the input. I'll then take the XLR signal directly to one track and print the miked signal. I use the AKG D 112 or the Electro Voice RE-20 to mike the bass cabinet near the bottom of the speaker, below the cone. This gives me the flexibility to blend the direct signal a little lower during mixdown, which I find adds full body to the bass sound.

This is a method I used when producing Randy Coven's new album featuring Leslie West. For solo bass tracks, it adds a wonderful depth of sound to the bass and gives the engineer flexibility when mixing. You can also do a nice stereo pan with the two signals, enabling you to EQ and affect the signals differently.

Most of these mics aren't terribly expensive. Prices can range anywhere from $200 to $1,500, which is worth it when it comes to achieving great guitar tones in your recordings. To be quite honest, I find that many artists tend to fall back on the less expensive and reliable SM57, especially after trying other mics. I always find that by experimenting you get the best results; hence multi-miking is a great avenue for covering the bases. Often you may find yourself liking the sound of two mics combined, but when soloed, the sound may not be as good or vice versa.

Also, keep in mind how the guitar tracks sit in the song. Spending a lot of time getting a huge overdriven guitar tone for a reggae song may not be the right direction. All of us have been in that boat sometime or another—working diligently on recording the best tone for the guitar part, only to realize that the guitar sounds great but does not fit the track at all. However, these mics will give you the tools for getting your guitar tones recorded. So when it comes to mics, think in terms of a producer as well.

Geoff Gray: Studio Guru

One of my mentors in studio recording was a wonderful guy named Geoff Gray, who owned Far and Away Studios in New York. I remember graduating from the Center for the Media Arts and finding work as an assistant engineer in his studio back in 1989. I learned quite a bit about studio recording and producing musicians during my tenure with Geoff. Since then, he has relocated Far and Away Studios to Boulder, Colorado, and continues to work with many different artists. He especially enjoys working with new acts and helping them create the best recordings possible. To Geoff, building good relationships with his clients has always been key, and many have become longtime friends.

When Geoff was in town, he stopped by Jungle Room Studios for a chat. In addition to working on mixes with me at the studio for the album *Fretworx*, he gave me the lowdown on Far and Away Studios and some of his favorite techniques for recording guitar.

How did you come up with the design of your studio? Were there any other studios that influenced you?

I remembered the first time I walked into the Power Station/Avatar Studio A and thought, "This is the most sonically and visually comfortable room I've ever been in." I wanted to create that in Colorado. We used indigenous pine and brought the outside to the inside—Rich Eberhardt came up with the overall design.

They don't make Martins and Strats and Les Pauls out of carpet. Wood just sounds great for a recording environment. The studio houses 17-foot ceilings, natural light, stunning views of the Flatirons (rock formations near Boulder), three iso areas, and a live echo chamber prefaced by a tube two-track Ampex.

Can you share your miking techniques with us for both amps and acoustic guitars?

We have various amp rooms and, depending on the size of the room, I vary the mics. Generally in the smaller areas, I go to a 57 or 58 off-axis and close to the grill. We use the big room often for overdubs, and that is perfect for the Royer 122s back about 18 inches. Unlike the amp booths, we encourage leakage from that room. The Royers are bidirectional, so I have to be cautious of the player standing nearby and stomping on pedals.

For example, in the case of Sammy Dee Morton's record [*Business Is Business*], he didn't want to use headphones, so we had the Fender in the big room poking out of the iso booth. I used a 57 and 58 to hedge my bets—we chose the 58. On the bass amp we used an EV RE20 on the big speakers and a Sennheiser 421 on the 10s. This was also live in the room 12 feet from Sammy's amp. We printed the drums in the same room, too.

With acoustic guitars, a DPA 4041 near the sound hole is amazing. This is an omni with a twist. If the acoustic is a major part of the song, I always use two Neumann KM 184s: one pointed up toward the bridge, back 15 inches or so, and the other pointed near the neck joint, also about that far back. I also like mono guitar accompanied with a mono Nashville-tuned Taylor miked up with a DPA or KM 184 near the neck joint.

Do you use digital or analog for recording? What is your setup?

We use a hybrid of Pro Tools HD and a Studer two-inch. We have the two-inch outs normalled to the HD ins so that I can have both digital and analog. Guitars generally get recorded directly to Pro Tools through Sony DMX converters but go through an old LA-2A, or LA-3As in the case of two acoustic mics. I love old Symetrix 202 mic pres for all guitars. We have API 312s that sound just great for all guitars—sometimes it's the Neve 1095s. During mixdown, I love the Neve 1095 EQs and the old API 550As. Shelving with the APIs on acoustics is a beautiful thing.

What mics do you use to record guitar?

I think a 57 is just great, the Royers are amazing in the right circumstances, a 421 on a cab is fun, and the DPAs never cease to amaze. The DPA 4023s in the ORTF pattern back from the cab are shocking. I'll often combine the 57 with the Royer but try to keep them on the same speaker in a multispeaker cab so that I don't have phase nightmares if I use them both.

Do you have a favorite can't-live-without guitar processor that you use?

Eventide Harmonizers are my favorite. We have three, and they all have different stock programs. For a Haas effect, I use the 949; for delays and sick effects, I use the H3000s. We have oddities that we sometimes dust off, like an Acousticomputer, MXR Flanger/ Doubler, Effectron Delays, and tape delays to chambers.

Chuck Loeb: Jazz Shredder

Chuck Loeb may not be a household guitar name; however, he has earned his weight in excellence as a jazz guitarist and studio musician. From his beginnings with the Stan Getz band, where he composed much of the band's repertoire, to replacing Larry Carlton in the well-known smooth jazz band Fourplay, Chuck has proven himself to be a versatile guitarist, composer, and producer.

Among Chuck's high moments were his days in the band Steps Ahead, with Michael Brecker, Michael Mainieri, Peter Erskine, and Victor Bailey. This returned him to the festivals and stages of the jazz world and rekindled his desire to focus on his own music. In 1988, after nearly 10 years of intense studio work, he made the decision to develop his own recording career. Since then, he has released seven solo records and has been a studio gun for hire for decades. I recently worked with Chuck on *Guitar Masters, Volume 3 & 4: Les Paul Dedication*, where he was a guest on two tracks and blew me away with his precision and pure jazz chops. It's no wonder he is Larry Carlton's successor in Fourplay.

Congratulations on your latest release with Fourplay's *Let's Touch the Sky*. What is your typical setup, guitar, amp, pedals, et cetera? Were there any particular artists or songs at the time that influenced you?

My Sadowsky guitars, of course: the solid body Strat model, the semihollow with the Bigsby bridge, and the Jazz Box. My pedal/amp setup has actually changed from the recording to now as we tour the album.

For the recording, I was using a Roland GT-10 with an Xotic AC Plus + Booster Over-drive pedal running stereo into two Fender Blues DeVille amplifiers.

Also, on some things I went direct using the Line 6-Pod Farm and Amp Farm, depending on what the tune called for. Performing live, I am using the Line 6 M13 Stompbox Modeler with a Moollon booster pedal in front. I guess I was referencing the first Fourplay CD from 1991 mostly for production values, sounds, et cetera. I used Nathan East's Martin 00018, a gift from Eric Clapton, on the acoustic stuff and Mike Miller's flamenco (no name) nylon.

How did the process go? Were the guitar parts written in the studio or already laid out between Bob and you? How were your guitar parts juxtaposed to Bob's keys?

It mostly worked out by both of us having worked together a bunch, as well as both being used to playing on a lot of other guitar/keyboard records. Bob is the ultimate musician, so he made it easy for me, too.

What microphones were used to record the guitar parts? Did you guys record in a studio or in home studios? Take us through a little bit of the recording process and the gear.

We did the record at Castle Oaks Studio in Los Angeles, and I believe the mic we used on the amps were Shure 57s, the old standby. I am a "whatever works" guy in the studio, so I went back and forth between amps, direct, acoustics, et cetera. I am not a live take purist either. I will punch and punch till we get it exactly right...no apologies there.

You have been a very successful solo jazz artist through the years. Can you tell us how working with a band like Fourplay changed your approach in making records and writing songs?

Well, when thinking of each of the guys in the band, certain ideas sprang to mind when I was writing my tunes. I have been a huge fan of both the group and the individuals for so long, it was like falling off a log, really. One thing that impressed me was that of the four songs I submitted to the project, the guys chose the most challenging and adventurous ones. Then they *killed* on them. The biggest change for me is to be able to relax and let others make the decisions sometimes. Fourplay is a truly democratic band.

On your solo recordings, what is your typical recording setup and how do you go about recording your guitar tones today in our digital world?

I do a lot of recording of guitar going direct and using plug-ins. As I mentioned, I like the Line 6 stuff a lot, but I also use Logic's system and the Eleven stuff sometimes. I use amps, too, but my frame of reference is what Jaco Pastorius once said to me about his sound: "It's in your hands, man."

The sound is really in the player's hands—literally.

Do you have a favorite can't-live-without guitar processor/effects that you use on your scores?

There are many, but I always go back to my CAE preamp for the super clean sound, and I have a new pre called Tube Top from Japan. I love the Roland GT 10 and Line 6 M13 for quick and easy setups at live gigs and festivals, where we only get a line check. The real world will make you a pragmatist quickly!

What projects are you working on currently?

I just finished my new CD, which is an organ trio project featuring Pat Bianchi on organ (kicking the bass pedals *to death*!) and Harvey Mason on drums. Harvey played with all the organ masters, including organ god Jimmy Smith, so I had a pretty awesome team! I also just finished up producing the new Michael Franks CD. Next fall I will be working on a solo guitar CD and a DVD with excerpts and lessons.

Anything you'd like to add, any guitar recording tips or advice?

Just the age-old advice: Play the guitar as much as you can, and after you've learned from the masters, do your best to find your own path to guitar enlightenment.

Oh, and one more thing: Don't get too locked into one axe, or pedal, or amp—whatever works in any given situation is *cool*!

James Ryan: Tone from Down Under

Another one of my favorite guitarists to use is the Australian hotshot James Ryan. James has been a gun for hire with Men at Work and performed with Shania Twain and Ronan Keating. He is also a Roland/Boss clinician and Fender endorsee, and he has been teaching guitar for over 10 years. I have used James on the *Guitar Master Series* to the *Classic Rock* collection releases. One of the great things about James is his progressive approach to guitar. His solo release "Blown" was a creative mixture of shred guitar and electronica beats.

This is something near and dear to my heart. I spearheaded a group called Asphalt Jungle, which really experimented with drum-n-bass and breakbeat rhythms combining various amounts of healthy guitar tones, tweaked and tortured to the utmost. Asphalt Jungle started in the mid-'90s and received excellent response from the TV and film music community, having been used for soundtracks on MTV, ABC-TV, and various film projects, such as "The First 20 Million," directed by Mick Jackson. Yes, Jeff Beck and Joe Satriani had experimented with this style, but unfortunately their fan base was so tuned into their previous signature releases that they just didn't understand the new music style.

James explains his recording setup for the tracks "Psycho Cycle" and "Monday Blues" that appeared on *Guitar Masters, Volume 3 & 4: Les Paul Dedication*.

What is your typical setup, guitar, amp, pedals, et cetera, when recording? Are there any particular artists or songs that influence you these days?

I use a variety of amps depending on the parts. My Marshall JCM800 is a great go-to rock amp. I also have an Egnater TOL 100 head, which has some great tones. I only plug in the pedals I need for each track, so usually I would have an overdrive, such as the T-Rex Mudhoney or Ulbrick 12 axe, and maybe a modulation effect (Electro Harmonics Small Stone phaser is one of my absolute favorites) and probably a wah pedal at the front. I constantly reference my favorite artists for tone ideas. Currently, I've been going through a heavy Vinnie Moore phase, but I still look to Stevie Ray Vaughan for the ultimate Strat tone, and no one could get more amazing sounds out of one guitar than Roy Buchanan. I've also been getting into Philip Sayce, who has a huge organic rocking Strat tone.

How does the process go when recording guitar parts? Are they written in the studio or already laid?

Sometimes I have a very clear idea. But I also have tons of unfinished tracks where I haven't been able to find the right parts or sounds ... yet!

What is your recording setup? What microphones do you find as your favorites? Take us through a little bit of the recording process and the gear.

I use Cubase, although I also have a Pro Tools setup. I recently bought a Universal Audio LA-610 preamp/compressor that is fantastic for guitars and bass; it has a very thick sound. I also have a Focusrite ISA 430, which is an amazing channel strip—very comprehensive. The compressor is a real slammer! Mic-wise, I'm usually happy with the good old 57 or Audix i5 into the UA610. Depending on the track, if there's enough space, I'll use my RØDE NT2 condenser to grab some room sound and compress the hell out of it.

Since I don't stick to a particular amp sound, I also don't use the same mic techniques or positions. I think it's better each time to start fresh, obviously using the knowledge that you have previously gained.

What first attracted you to being a guitar instrumentalist? How did you accomplish your vision of getting your guitar tone recorded?

My dad is the biggest rock guitar music lover of all time, so from a very young age I was absorbing the sound of Kiss, Sabbath, Iron Maiden, and Ozzy and also a lot of blues. So guitar solos were implanted in my subconscious. Then in the late '80s, when I was learning to play, there were so many incredible players. I got right into the kings of shred: Yngwie, Steve Vai, Vinnie Moore, and Tony MacAlpine. I still love that stuff.

As far as recorded sounds go, I have my good and bad days. My main thing is just to try anything and everything. To be honest, I've been using a lot of modeling amps and simulators, especially the Digidesign Eleven Rack. It's really quite amazing. The Fender G-Dec is another killer little amp for an instantly great direct recording tone.

Since your days, with Men at Work, you have been a very active guitarist. Can you tell us how your stint with the band helped your guitar playing and writing?

Playing with Men at Work certainly introduced me to a new network of people in the industry and helped me get more attention and therefore more calls. Also, working with the incredible Colin Hay and Greg Ham really raised the bar and made me want to achieve more from my career and become a better all-around musician.

Do you have a favorite can't-live-without guitar processor/effects that you use?

My favorite effects are my customized Electro-Harmonix Small Stone, my Roger Mayer Voodoo Vibe, and my McCon-O-Wah.

What projects are you working on currently?

I've been producing and mixing tracks for a songwriter in New York named Larry Dvoskin.

I am also currently working on some video clips for a recent series of Fender guitar concerts. And as always, I'm sifting through the mega load of instrumental songs, riffs, and ideas to try to complete a new album. I'm also desperately trying to find the time to get my trio rehearsed, so we can do some shows.

Anything you'd like to add, any guitar recording tips or advice?

This might seem silly, but when it comes to tuners, you need to decide which one you want to use and stick to it for everything. In my studio, I have at least eight different tuners, including software versions, and they all seem to have slight variations, which can really mess with things by the time you've got a lot of tracks happening. On a similar subject, make sure your guitars and basses are set up and have accurate intonations, so you don't end up with tuning madness!

Chris Poland: Megadeth Torque

Chris Poland is probably best known as the former lead guitarist for Megadeth, during the group's early years, on the releases *Killing Is My Business ... and Business Is Good!* and *Peace Sells ... but Who's Buying?* He is actually much more than just what you hear on those records. Chris has an incredible flowing technique and a great dimension as a guitarist, which can be heard in his power trio OHM. I worked with Chris on a track called "Tarquinius Maximus," released on *Guitar Masters, Volume 3 & 4: Les Paul Dedication*, and it showcased some fantastic chops and tone that made the song a standout.

Even before his stint with Megadeth, Chris's clean, overdriven tone and legato phrasing made him instantly recognizable. His unique style can be partially attributed to an injury to his index finger on his fret hand. This injury forced him to develop a style that includes smoothly phrased passages and wide intervallic leaps. Chris was in a fusion band called the New Yorkers with Robby Pagliari on bass, Gar Samuelson on drums, and Gar's brother Stu playing guitar, along with various horn players. Their music has been described as being in the same vein as Return to Forever, Mahavishnu, and Brand X. Although the New Yorkers never recorded, demos and rehearsal recordings do exist.

In 1984, Megadeth hired Chris, replacing Kerry King of Slayer, who was temporarily filling in as lead guitarist. In 1985, Megadeth released their debut album *Killing Is My Business ... and Business Is Good!* on the small independent label Combat Records. Though Dave Mustaine and Chris shared much of the lead guitar work equally, it was obvious that Chris had easily incorporated his fusion style into this genre of music.

In 1986, the rights for *Peace Sells ... but Who's Buying?* were bought by Capitol Records, and it was released with the support only a major record label could provide. The success of *Peace Sells* found Chris and Megadeth among the metal heavyweights of the day: Iron Maiden, Judas Priest, and Metallica. Chris's playing can be heard on such metal classics as "Peace Sells ... but Who's Buying?," "Devil's Island," and "Good Mourning/Black Friday."

Let's go back to the recording of Megadeth's, *Peace Sells ... but Who's Buying?* What was your typical setup, guitar, amp, pedals, et cetera? Were there any particular artists or songs at the time that influenced you?

I was using a BC Rich Warlock at the time with a Rocktron and a post-Plexi '75 Marshall. I also had a Twin reverb in the studio. I didn't use any pedals in my setup at the time. I was listening to a lot of fusion back then as well—Weather Report, Jeff Beck, Mahavishnu, et cetera. I grew up on Hendrix, Clapton, and Zeppelin as well, so they influenced my playing.

How did the process go? Were the guitar parts written in the studio or already laid out between Dave and you? How were your guitar parts juxtaposed to Dave's?

With *Peace Sells...* we were playing those songs on three successive tours before we even went in to record, so we really had the songs down and developed. Dave wrote the music, but we contributed ideas on arrangements here and there in the studio. Dave and I had unison guitar parts and would trade off on leads for certain songs.

What microphones were used to record the guitar parts? Do you remember the studio gear and producer? Was it recorded and mixed at the same studio?

I think we had 57s or 421s. We didn't have esoteric mics. Randy Burns was a great producer and really knew how to record the type of music we were playing. The drums were recorded at the Music Grinder in Hollywood, and we did some of the overdubs at Mad Dog Studios in Venice, California.

Since the Megadeth days, you have been a successful and active fusion guitarist with your band OHM. Can you tell us how you formed the band and why you went back to fusion? Also, how did your experience with Megadeth help you in your fusion playing and writing?

I was playing in a few bands around LA in the late '90s and just wasn't enjoying it. I knew Robby Pagliari (OHM's bassist) for years, as we played in a fusion band called the New Yorkers in the late '70s/early '80s, when I first moved to LA. Gar Samuelson (Megadeth drummer) was also in that band on drums. With OHM we really wanted to play the music we like to play. My experience with Megadeth really taught me about the music business and didn't really influence me from a musical direction standpoint, although I really enjoyed playing that music and the challenge of it.

What is your typical recording setup and how do you go about recording your guitar tones today in our digital world?

This depends on the studio. In my personal studio, we record mostly live and overdub some guitars. Right now I have a Tascam M2600 MK2 board, but I will be getting a new Toft board soon. When I do studio sessions, I go to my friend Randy Pevler's Pro Tools studio.

Do you have a favorite can't-live-without guitar processor/effects that you used on your scores?

That is a tough question. Right now I would have to say my Yamaha D1500 delay and DC1210 Chorus are my faves.

What projects are you working on currently?

I just finished a record with Chicago sax player Frank Catalano (he played with Miles Davis and Santana), bassist Sean O'Bryan Smith (a Nashville session ace), and drummer Jim Gifford (a Chicago session ace). It will be coming out on a label based out of Chicago. I am also doing a new OHMPHREY disc in a few weeks, with Robby (OHM bassist), and Jake, Joel, and Kris from Umphrey's McGee here at my studio. After that we start recording the new OHM CD, which has been written for some time. Now we just have to record it, and we are thinking of doing it live in the studio. A lot of stuff coming out in 2011 and 2012.

Anything you'd like to add—any guitar recording tips or advice?

Use your ears and don't follow the "rules" of recording. If you like how you are sounding, then record it, so you don't lose what is happening at that moment. I really would like to also promote live recording, as I have been really feeling lately how much more energy there is in a live context. Thank you to all the fans out there and awesome musicians and projects I have worked with and on over the past few years. I have been having a lot of fun.

Hal Lindes: Unsung Hero

Hal Lindes is perhaps best known as the former guitarist of the British rock band Dire Straits. His distinctive sound and influence can be heard on such landmark albums as *Love Over Gold* and *Alchemy*. Having had the privilege of working with Hal, I can say he is one of the most underrated guitarists of our time. His true understanding of the guitar and all it holds in tone and passion is truly remarkable. I have worked with Hal for a number of years on the *Guitar Master Series* and *Fretworx*. He is always my first choice when I desire a guest guitarist and my first-call man of the hour.

So it's no wonder he is in great demand as a musician, an arranger, and a producer. Hal's talent for writing from the heart is wonderfully evident in his poignant and evocative film score for *The Boys Are Back*, starring Clive Owen and directed by Scott Hicks. Hal is currently working on some pre-records and musical arrangements for the Warner Brothers feature film *The Lucky One*, starring Zac Efron and, again, directed by Scott Hicks. Hal has composed music for a variety of film and TV series, and his scores have won many awards, including a Royal Television Society award for the BAFTA-nominated film *Reckless* and a TRIC award for Best TV Theme Music for *Thieftakers*. But beyond all of the accolades, Hal has something that many musicians lack: heart and soul!

Let's go back to the recording of Dire Straits _Brothers in Arms_. What was your typical setup, guitar, amp, pedals, et cetera? Were there any particular artists or songs at the time that influenced you?

Unless a song had an obvious call for a certain guitar, I would generally start out with either the early '60s Cream Strat or one of the Schecter Strats through a 1984 Fender Concert RI (2 × 10). If a different amp tonality was required, I would go for either the 1957 Fender Tweed Twin or my stage rig Boogie and Marshall 4 × 12 cab.

My other guitars were the 1980 blue Schecter Strat (from Mark with the inscription "Play It Hal, Mark" on the neck plate), the "Alchemy" 1982 Fullerton RI '52 Telecaster with gray top pickups, the "Twisting By the Pool" '60s Red Gretsch Jet Firebird (one of the first production guitars to incorporate active circuitry), a 1955 translucent Cream Fender Strat, a 1952 Blonde Gibson ES-5, a 1974 Sunburst Telecaster Deluxe, and three of my guitars Mark used to play onstage: a 1982 black Fullerton RI '57 Strat, a 1972 Black Rickenbacker 425, and a 1968 white Gibson 3 pickup SG.

For effects, I was running through a BOSS SCC-700 Foot Controller system, patching through to a rack-mounted Roland 31 Band Graphic, Roland SRE-555 Chorus Echo Unit, Roland SDE-300 Digital Delay, Yamaha E-1010 Analog Delay, Ernie Ball Volume Pedal, Vox Wah-Wah, MXR Compressor, MXR Phase 90, Boss Digital Delay, Boss Dimension C, and an MXR Micro Amp.

For acoustic work, I would generally use the 1972 Martin D-35, with the "Love Over Gold" 1982 Ovation Classical and the 1980 Custom-Legend XII and VI as alternatives to experiment with.

Before starting the rehearsals for _BIA_ [_Brothers in Arms_], Fender provided a host of Concert amps to test out, resulting in the selection of a killer-sounding tone machine that really stood out from the pack. Mark was also using that Concert initially while in the formative stages of shaping the tone for the "Money for Nothing" riff.

In terms of influences, at the time, I had just finished recording "Private Dancer" and playing some gigs with Tina Turner, which was quite an experience. I was also interested in the guitarist Ted Greene, managing to take some tuition from him after tracking Ted down in his eccentrically disheveled, vintage gear–strewn apartment in the San Fernando Valley, with the freeway flying past his window.

As a band we were listening to ZZ Top's _Eliminator_ and Pink Floyd's _The Wall_.

How did the process go? Were the guitar parts written in the studio or already laid out between Mark and you? How were your guitar parts juxtaposed to Mark's?

Prior to making _BIA_, all band rehearsals used to take place at Wood Wharf Rehearsal Studios in Greenwich, South London, situated next to the Cutty Sark overlooking the River Thames. It was a rough-and-tumble place, with an organic vibe that was highly conducive to the creative process. At low tide, the banging of hammers against barges in need of repair was heard between the pauses of the band's music, and at day's end the red sun would set like a fireball over the river.

This changed with *BIA*, with the initial rehearsals taking place at Phil Manzanera's studio in Virginia Waters in Surrey.

As with the past albums, the prerecording routine process remained pretty much the same, with Mark running down a tune, usually on his Ovation Adamas, while the rest of us would scribble down the chord changes. If Mark had a specific part in mind, he would spend some time with the player and craft the part. At some point, the song would be played by the band, and Mark would usually hear something in a part one of the musicians was working on and spend time with that player refining it. My goal was to find a guitar part that would support and complement Mark's guitar performance.

Little by little the songs would get shaped and fine-tuned before the band relocated to Air Studios in Montserrat, where engineer-coproducer Neil Dorfsman first heard the songs performed live by the band. The lineup at the time was Mark and myself on guitars, John Illsley on bass, Terry Williams on drums, and Alan Clark and newcomer Guy Fletcher on keyboards.

What microphones were used to record the guitar parts? Do you remember the studio gear and producer? Was it recorded and mixed at the same studio?

The main microphones were mostly Neumann U 67s, AKG 451s, and Shure SM57s. The amps were miked with an SM57 on the speaker, a U 67 slightly back, and one or two overhead mics to capture the room ambience.

For the acoustic parts, I would use the 1972 Martin D-35 I have owned since my school days and still very much use today. (This D-35, along with a 1975 Martin D-28, were prominently featured on the musical score for the Scott Hicks film *The Boys Are Back*.)

As far as I can remember, the acoustic was miked with an AKG 451 pointing toward the 12th fret and a Neumann U 67 pointing between the bridge and the sound hole, with both mics positioned a foot or two away from the guitar.

Air Montserrat had a gorgeous-sounding Neve 8078 console, custom ordered and specifically built for Sir George Martin, who was around, visiting the studio, at the time of recording *BIA*.

The music was recorded on a Sony 3324 Digital 24-track recorder, which the band had purchased specifically for the project. Additional recordings and mixing took place at the Power Station in New York. The building was originally a Consolidated Edison power plant, then a sound studio where the television game show *Let's Make a Deal* was filmed, and by the early '80s became the mecca of recording studios.

Since the Dire Straits days, you have been a very successful and active film composer. Can you tell us how the guitar is incorporated into your scores?

When used against moving images, the guitar is a unique and powerfully evocative voice with a direct emotional connection, which is honest in an unmanipulative way.

When appropriate, I strive for the guitar to drive the musical piece, utilizing more traditional orchestral instrumentation to support underneath the guitar, giving weight and scale to the music that feature films require.

I tend to lean more toward the acoustic aspects of the guitar scoring, incorporating four- and eight-string ukuleles, Dobro, mandolin, charango, three-quarter-size acoustics, classical nylon and 12-string guitars into the mix.

What is your typical recording setup and how do you go about recording your guitar tones today in our digital world?

My acoustic guitar of choice for film scores is a 1975 Martin D-28 with its fat, baseball type of neck and sustain that is somewhat reminiscent of a grand piano.

An old Gefell UM-70 microphone is positioned between the bridge and sound hole, about a foot or two away from the Martin. The mic goes to a vintage Neve 1272 mic pre, then through to an Apogee Rosetta 800 converter running at 48k/24 bit.

While screening the film on a 55-inch LED monitor, I record a number of performances, usually without a click. I look for the performance that helps the image just pop off the screen, which, surprisingly, may be the performance with a few imperfections in it, like loose timing, uneven velocities, or a razzing note. There is something about an imperfect performance that can sometimes bring out the vulnerability and character of a film scene.

The one rule I've learned as a film composer over the years is that there are no rules to film scoring. Each film has its own particular quirks attached to it, and if the composer can remain open enough, then the film image will create the music for him.

Do you have favorite can't-live-without guitar processor/effects that you used on your scores?

Good question. The mantra is big, clean, and warm, which the Gefell UM-70 and the Neve 1272 certainly help to achieve, but that's not to say that another combination of mics and mic pres won't yield an unexpected but equally desirable result.

In my case, it's probably more about the tools that are needed to help inspire and create a film score than the actual make and manufacture of the individual item. Apart from the mic and mic pre, things like capos, slides, soft, hard, felt, and finger picks, bows, hammers, and a variety of acoustic instruments are essential items.

What projects are you working on currently?

I'm currently working on some pre-records and musical arrangements for the Warner Brothers film *The Lucky One* starring Zac Efron and directed by Scott Hicks.

I'm also putting the finishing touches on an acoustic guitar CD for EMI called *Guitar Heart*.

Anything you'd like to add—any guitar recording tips or advice?

Shake it up, get inspired, be adventurous and most importantly, enjoy yourself. After all, it's only rock-n-roll!

Doug Doppler: Channeling the Guitar Hero

Favored Nations artist Doug Doppler is now a certified guitar hero through his involvement with the PlayStation 2 video game *Guitar Hero Encore: Rocks the '80s*. Doppler became part of the

WaveGroup Sound production house family in 2007, contributing six tracks to the '80s version of the multimillion unit–selling *Guitar Hero* franchise. Serving as the game's Furious Fretwork Encore is his remake of Extreme's "Play with Me"—a difficult track to play and a perfect showcase for Doppler's amazing guitar skills. In fact, on YouTube, videos of people playing to Doppler's cut have already generated more than 100,000 hits. A former student of Joe Satriani, Doug was chosen by his former teacher to preside over teaching duties at the studio in Berkeley, California. It's a no-brainer that Ibanez endorsed Doug, asking him to write a promotional song for the Zero Resistance tremolo from their new S Series guitars, which Doug titled "Zero Gravity."

The Doppler Effect

For the song "Zero Gravity," Doug used an Ibanez S470 into an M-Audio Black Box set on a Dual Rectifier model. The Black Box is a creative tool for the guitarist, combining amp modeling, drum machine features, and an audio interface for computer-based recording. It boasts some of the greatest guitar amps of all time—including the Fender Bassman, Fender Deluxe, Fender Twin, Vox AC30, Marshall JTM 45, Marshall Plexi, Marshall JCM 2000, Hiwatt DR-103, Soldano SLO-100, Mesa Boogie Maverick, Mesa Boogie Dual Rectifier, and Bogner Uberschall—and programmable drive and tone controls, not to mention 99 built-in drum patterns.

Doug adds, "At various points on the track I introduce various effects like delay and chorus, all of which originated in the Black Box as opposed to using plug-ins. The Black Box, like many modeling devices, shines in its plug-and-play nature."

Digital Domain

According to Doug, "I'm a Pro Tools shop, and this track was cut with my Digi001, which has since been upgraded to 002. I do a lot of session work these days, and have become a bit of a mad scientist in the edit window." A good thing to point out is that guitarists have become much more proficient at recording their own tracks and editing them together through the convenience of cut, copy, and paste functions. This is especially true with the editing procedures of Pro Tools. Doug goes on to recall, "Oddly enough, on this song, I didn't edit the guitar tracks at all. It was written and recorded in one day, with the exception of the bass track, which was added a few days later."

Doug continues, "One of the track's cool incidentals was the drum loops—most loopheads would recognize them from Garage Band. What was fun was how I used them in the track. I cut the track to a drum machine beat and then took the BPM into Garage Band to grab some loops and set them up along the timeline in a linear array. Then I imported them into Pro Tools and sliced and diced and did some stacking as well. What's cool about this approach is that you get an instantaneous palette to work from instead of loading a bunch of samples and trying them over a section, one at a time."

This is an important tip to remember when working with drum programming: Always have enough samples to access while programming, so you don't have to stop and load samples and break the creative flow. Nothing is as bad as stopping and looking for a certain drum fill through hundreds of samples and the subsequent loss of concentration.

Gravity at Work

Rob Nishida, head of artist relations at Ibanez, sent Doug a new S470 guitar to try out during the recording of "Zero Gravity." "The funny thing is that the fine tuner accidentally broke, and it took the low E down to B while the rest of the guitar stayed almost perfectly in tune. The point being, if you play a power chord shape on the low E with that tuning, you end up with octaves, and that's how that track came about—me fiddling around in the studio. In terms of the sound design, once I had the composition in place, I picked the effect treatments I wanted to use for each section. This song is really a tremolo demonstration and some effects sound better for certain types of bar work than others. I did a little experimenting and found what seemed to work. The track is an interesting blend of the creative and experimental, which for me is one of the greatest pleasures in the digital domain."

A great characteristic of the digital domain is the endless creative possibilities it affords. Inspired by the S470 and the Black Box, Doug was able to call up any desired amp tone combined with Pro Tools to perfect "Zero Gravity." This is a perfect marriage of the digital domain and the devastating riffs of the *Guitar Hero*.

3 Recording Gear

Compression can be a very subtle effect, especially on electric guitar, or it can be used in extreme fashions. There are many things to consider when using a compressor on a guitar. For instance, when miking a tube amp that is overdriven, the tubes are actually compressing the signal, so there is really no need to compress when recording. But on the other hand, when recording an acoustic guitar live with a mic, there are many sound transients that affect the dynamics of the guitar strings. Hence compressing the track helps to control the musical integrity of the performance to your recording source.

"Seven Moons was recorded in London at Intimate Studios. We used a Shure 57 a few inches from each combo through a Summit DCL 200 (stereo valve comp) and the Urie 1176."

—Robin Trower

"I used a Neumann KM 184, pointing down the neck of the guitar, toward the sound hole. Right in front of me, I used a handmade mic that a friend of Kim's had designed, similar to an old Telefunken 251 centered to the sound hole about eight inches in front of me."

—Tommy Emmanuel

"Also, EQ plays a vital role. I always keep a pair of C14s and a pair of 414s [mics] spread apart in the corners of the room. This is mixed into the sound at various levels, depending on the desired effect."

—Steve Vai

Compressors and Guitars

It is interesting to see how different each one of these guitar heroes approaches compression. Trower creates his classic tone by using the Urei 1176, while Tommy takes the audiophile route by using the pristine clarity of the boutique Pendulum Audio compressor. As for the shred master, Mr. Vai takes the dual approach of using both analog and digital compression, using the Waves L1 for its renowned transparency and punch. All great choices. Still, there are many other fantastic compressors on the market to try, both vintage and new, when recording and mixing guitar tracks.

Urei LA-4

One of my all-time favorites is the optical Limiter Urei LA-4 (see Figure 3.1), probably one of the best compressors for the guitar. It is extremely transparent, very easy to use, and very flexible. The difference between the LA-4 and its predecessor, the LA-3A, is the added Ratio control, without the added confusion of Attack and Release controls introduced on newer optical limiters. Any tech will tell you that the whole beauty of Optos in general is their simplicity. In fact, it shines on just about any stringed instrument, whether bass, acoustic guitar, electric guitars, even Rhodes and the organ. The best trait of this limiter is that it is actually difficult to make it sound bad. I have a pair that I had recapped (capacitors replaced), and the quality of sound that it produces on a lead guitar and solo is mind-blowing. It handles the guitar signal flawlessly, without losing the tone or dynamics. This is something of utmost importance: *You don't want to disturb the tone you worked so hard to get recorded!* I generally use it on various guitars during a mix to control everything at the final stage.

Figure 3.1   Urei LA-4.

Purple Audio MC77

Do you like the classic FET sound of the Urei 1176? Well think of the MC77 (see Figure 3.2) as an 1176 on steroids. This bad purple monster kicks some serious booty! It has the identical controls of the 1176 but a fatter squash. Just like the 1176, the front panel has two large knobs, two small knobs, a meter, and two columns of buttons. The large knobs adjust input and output level; the small knobs adjust attack and release times. And yes, it has the all-buttons capability to really get that crush for drums. In fact, when I record drums, I put a mono room mic through it and push all the buttons in to get a pseudo Bonham sound. But I love using it on guitar—especially crunchy rhythm guitar to give it some girth. It also shines on bass, giving it some presence in a mix, without the muddy effect.

Figure 3.2   Purple Audio MC77.

I usually track using the MC77 on rhythm acoustic guitar to control the transients, while bringing out the attack of the pick on the strings. This is a bit more colored-sounding than the LA-4, but used in the right way, it has wonderful results in a mix.

Anthony DeMaria 1500

The brilliance of Mr. DeMaria comes all out in this fantastic-sounding limiter. Similar to the LA-4, the 1500 utilizes Opto attenuators to create "invisible" compression (see Figure 3.3). It's a two-channel, all-tube design with phenomenal dynamic range. It boasts eight vacuum tubes, giving it unmistakable richness and depth. This unit has an incredible cross-platform use, from being a beefy buss compressor to limiting individual instruments. I love using this on guitars; the tubes add fullness without coloring the signal. On acoustic guitars—fuhgeddaboudit! It makes them stand out with a creaminess of tube circuitry.

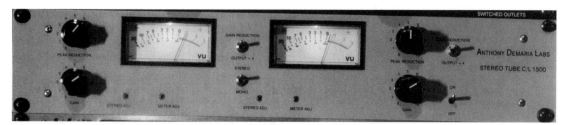

Figure 3.3 Anthony DeMaria 1500.

I usually route two rhythm guitar tracks through it in stereo to achieve a warm presence in the mix. The only thing you have to be mindful of is your headroom; you can't push it like the 1176 without getting undesirable distortion. So for those of you who record directly in a DAW with amp modeling plug-ins, this would be the ideal compressor for you to have at mixdown, to warm up that cold digital signal.

Anthony DeMaria 670

This is the Rolls-Royce of limiters; some may call it the Holy Grail of compression. It is a reproduction of the classic Fairchild 670 (see Figure 3.4). It is truly a sonic beast and sounds unbelievable. On guitars it adds such an incredible punch and clarity delivered from the 18 tubes and 14 transformers, really putting the "F" in *fat*! It's handmade like a tank with "military strength"; every detail has been scrutinized to perfection to re-create the original. Surprisingly easy to use, it has four control knobs, input gain, ratio, DC threshold, and a fine-tune threshold. These last two controls are interactive with each other, which is a fantastic idea. You can set your threshold point and then use the fine-tune knob to dial in a compression point you are seeking. The saying "a little goes a long way" is very true when using the ADL 670 on guitars. You don't need to see the VU meters moving about to get the compression effect. On rhythm guitar the limiter gives a punch, especially if you have a real crunch tone. But the great thing about this limiter is that it delivers a velvety smooth sound that creates fullness in the track for guitar.

Figure 3.4 Anthony DeMaria 670.

Overall, I believe the trick to understanding compression and how it works is experimenting with different compressors on guitar and seeing how they interact with the track. Some compressors just don't do it for a guitar track, no matter how hard you try. Keep in mind that compressors are designed to keep the dynamics under control in a track, so be very careful not to overuse it on guitars, or you'll hear the pumping, or what is known as "breathing," of the guitar, which means you should back off the compressor.

The most important factor for me when choosing a compressor for a guitar is how it will enhance the guitar without coloration to the tone. There are some guitar tracks you may never need to compress, such as a high-gain lead tone. The tubes of the amp have already done the compression, and the higher the gain, the less dynamics, because the preamp gain stage in the amp is doing just that—compressing the guitar tone with the gain sound. Be careful to always monitor the VU meter during gain reduction as well, because it is very easy to overdo it. Generally –3 dB is a safe place to be. Use your ears, and you will be fine.

Microphone Preamps

In the past decade there has been a huge surge of microphone preamps, everything from simple tube-driven to all discrete Class A circuitry. This may be a response to the analog days, when all studios had preamps built into their recording consoles, so no one really gave outboard mic pres a second thought, unless they were looking for a particular flavor. Today it seems that more and more people are becoming "in the box" warriors, and finding the perfect mic pre is crucial to the recording quality. Most of the preamps in computer audio interfaces don't cut it. Especially for guitar recording, you want a preamp to capture the tone of the instrument, not a thin digital replica that does not do the guitar tone justice. In the following quotes, some guitar heroes explain how they record monster tones.

"We recorded all analog on an SSL 4000 G/G+, 72 inputs, 16 E modules and Neve 1081 mic pre/EQ."

—Zakk Wylde

"We used a Neve 8068-Customized 64 input with a GML automation and a couple of 24-track analog Studer recording machines, A800 and A827."

—Neal Schon

"The clean/arpeggiated tracks were close-miked with a Shure 57 on a 2 × 12 Line 6 cab. I recorded through a Focusrite ISA 430 preamp into Cubase, using the built-in high-quality converters."

—James Ryan (Men at Work)

Obviously, there are different approaches to recording, but Zakk and Neal prefer to record through the mic pres in a classic analog desk, which I also favor—but as I said, having a 32-channel classic Trident console at my fingertips tends to spoil me. However, I've done many sessions using the Universal Audio 2-610 and the LA-610 directly into Pro Tools and Logic with terrific results. Guitarist James Ryan utilizes a good signal chain, bypassing any analog mixer through one of the Focusrite pres into Cubase. Whichever mic pre you choose, I think it is important to get something that is not too colored and that retains the analog warmth of the guitar, which counterbalances the cold digital signal of DAW. I'll go over some of the more popularly used mic pres and see how they stack up for the shredder in you.

Neve 1081

Rupert Neve needs no introduction, but for those of you who are not familiar with the 1081, it is probably one of the most desirable mic pres in the recording world. It was originally designed in 1972 as the mic/line preamp and equalizer section for the Neve modular console. These consoles are still being used today on platinum-selling albums, and for good reason. Rupert himself won a technical Grammy from the National Academy of Recording Arts and Sciences for his contributions to outstanding technical significance in the recording field. The 1081 modules are still built by hand in Burnley, UK, under the mother company, AMS, in much the same manner as the original modules, using the original components, hand-wound transformers, and time-honed construction methods.

The 1081's magic is in its Neve equalization, which features effective high- and low-pass filters designed to separate unwanted signals. The flexibility of shaping your sound is so intuitive that creating curves and slopes can be achieved at a high artistic level. This explains the longtime love affair with the Neve recording console for the past 40 years. It is still an exceptional choice for recording guitars and is the original rock-n-roll preamp made to rock!

SSL 4000

Many consider this to be the Holy Grail of consoles because of its clarity and groundbreaking automation. Virtually all SSLs have been used on every pop album since the 1980s. Outside of the big-name studios that own one of these babies, purchasing one will certainly break the bank.

At close to $100,000 brand new, and with a vintage one costing a fortune to repair, you may want to just go the cost-effective route and purchase an SSL Mynx with 9K Series Mic Pre and Dynamics Modules. For a fraction of the price, you can still have the SSL legendary technology that is perfect as an interface with your favorite DAW.

SSL Mynx uses the identical circuit design and manufacturing of Duality and AWS 900+ consoles. The Mynx is a desktop mini X-Rack that allows you to load various X-Rack modules into two slots. The SSL Mic Pre module, with its compact size, is designed especially for the DAW user. The Mic Amp module has a great mic pre with 75 dB of gain, variable impedance control, phantom power and phase reverse line input with level control, front panel instrument input, and high- and low-pass filters. This is perfect for the guitarist who has a small home-studio setup. SSL has always been known for a non-coloring sound, with audiophile clarity.

Universal Audio LA-610

One of my favorite mic pres is the UA 610, because of its tube warmth that adds to the guitar. It especially shines when used in recording guitar directly to hard disk. And you have to dig those huge rotary knobs it sports.

The genius behind the 610, one of the first modular recording consoles in the world, was Bill Putnam, the man who has been aptly called "the father of modern recording." Interestingly enough, Putnam had several studios, including Universal Recording in Chicago and United/Western in Los Angeles, which used his early Universal Audio console designs.

The 610 was famous for its prominent preamplifier, featured on a plethora of classic recordings, from Frank Sinatra to Van Halen. The 610 Modular features variable gain and output levels, variable impedance switching, balanced line/Hi-Z inputs, and my favorite high- and low-shelving EQ. I find the EQ very useful in particular. It is subtle yet extremely musical and can shape a guitar tone nicely to sit in a track.

Focusrite ISA430

The 25-year-old British company Focusrite manufactures our last preamp. The shred maestro James Ryan's approach utilizes the ISA430 MkII, which has analog channel strip technology, bringing together all the classic designs in one rack unit. The mic preamp section has an impedance switching and "mic air" effect (a wire-wound inductor for increased spaciousness), three compressor options (VCA, Vintage Opto, and Opto Limit) combined with the compressed/uncompressed signal, and even a blend feature.

Routing and monitoring are important features on the ISA430, which allows you to listen (hone in on the frequency you wish to effect) on compressor, gate, and expander circuits. To round things off, the ISA430 has a unique phase cancellation–based de-esser circuit and an optional 24-bit/192-kHz high-performance stereo A-D converter, allowing you to retain your analog guitar signal into the digital domain. Focusrite has always been known for its digital clarity and multidynamic rack units.

Aside from the Neve 1081, these mic preamps are not terribly expensive, when you consider the high-priced boutique options out there in the recording retail world. Don't feel that you have to use some sort of guitar pod or a lame amp simulator plug-in to get your sound recorded. Purchase a good mic pre and a basic Shure 57 mic, and you'll be in business to record true guitar tone to your DAW. Believe me, there is nothing worse than hearing guitar parts recorded purely digital, thin and sterile—much like hearing drums recorded direct to hard disk. Take your time and get your sound together in the room before you record down.

Sometimes I see guitarists record both ways, which yields very good results. On one track they record a direct signal with a Line 6, and on another track they record a miked amp signal. One way to be sure of picking the right mic pre for you is to call a local rental company, such as SIR in New York, and rent a few pres for a day to see what floats your boat. This way you know what to buy, and you don't have to commit until you're positive of the result. Either way, get that guitar tone recorded and shred on!

Best Recording Amps

There are a lot of amps out there to choose from, but not all make good recording amps. I have always been a true believer that recording guitar doesn't have to be done at cripplingly loud levels. In fact, recording with lower wattage amps sometimes delivers a punchier tone. You metalheads scoff, but listen to the first Led Zeppelin album—great tone and hard hitting, and Page recorded it with small amps, such as the Supro amps with a Telecaster. Even Pete Townshend used a Mark I on the album *Who Are You*. So don't judge a book by its cover, as they say! Here are some of my favorite amps in the studio. Though let me preface this list with something that is as true as the fact that the sun will come out tomorrow—it's the player that makes the amp, meaning that the end-result tone comes from your *fingers* first!

Fender Twin Reverb

The Fender Twin Reverb (see Figure 3.5) is the classic amp with real mojo. It is wonderful for creating a cleaner tone, and when the Blackface circuitry is turned up, it gives a very nice, soft overdrive that is very musical. I remember always requesting these amps back in the day when I was touring the Jazz Festival venues in California. I'd use these with a 1960 Marshall cabinet— very effective. The amp also takes to subtle overdrive pedals, such as the Ibanez Tube King (see Figure 3.6), and really brings out those singing tubes. For studio duties it is fantastic! Pair it with a Shure 57, and it will sound wonderful. Or for added punch, you can mike the back of the amp, because it's open, and blend it in with the 57.

Hiwatt Bulldog Combo

I first used this amp years ago in a London recording studio during my solo career on Instinct Records. It came in a 1 × 12 combo cabinet and had such a huge sound. It would break up subtlety as you turned it up, but it cleaned up very nicely. I put an Ibanez Tube King pedal, which had an actual 12AX7 tube in it. The two were very happy together, producing a lush sweet

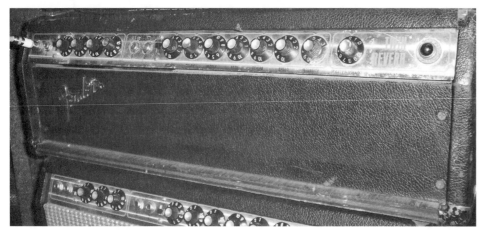

Figure 3.5 Fender Twin (cut down to a head).

Figure 3.6 Ibanez Tube King.

overdrive tone. The amp produced wonderful bell tones for clean octaves. We put a Beyerdynamic M 130 in front of the amp, and it captured all of the tone in the room. We had a bunch of amps in the room at the time, and the Hiwatt beat out the Vox, Fender, and Marshall. But you must realize that the amp you choose has to be dictated by the song and part you are playing.

Mesa Boogie Mark II Combo

The Mesa Boogie Mark II (see Figure 3.7) is one of my preferred amps for recording. You can get crystal-clean tones to heavily saturated overdrive that just absolutely sings like Santana. I found that the combos with EV 12-inch speakers are the best ones to own. To get that fantastic tone, you really have to push these amps, which can get pretty loud, so I use an attenuator to overdrive the power tubes and transformers without going deaf. The Weber Speaker Mass (www.tedweber.com) has an actual speaker motor built in that adds to the natural sound of the amp, as opposed to the others on the market that sound very sterile (see Figure 3.8). It also has Tone Stack controls, a multi-impedance switch, and a treble boost. The THD has a dB control and a Deep and Bright switch (see Figure 3.9).

Figure 3.7 Mesa Boogie Mark II.

Marshall JTM 45 Head

Hello, hello, hello! It doesn't get any better than the Marshall JTM 45 Head (see Figure 3.10), which has the best tone in the world. In case you're wondering, this came in a 2 × 12 combo that earned the name "the Bluesbreaker" because this is the amp Eric Clapton used on the famous album he did with John Mayall and the Bluesbreakers: *Bluesbreakers with Eric Clapton*, celebrated as one of the best British blues albums of the 1960s. The amp was born in Jim Marshall's London music store, where, as fate should have it, designers Ken Bran and Dudley Craven chose to put the British tube 12AX7 in the first stage of the amp's preamp section instead of the

Figure 3.8 Weber Mass.

Figure 3.9 THD Hot Plate.

Figure 3.10 Marshall JTM 45 Head.

12AY7 that was commonly used in the American Fender Bassman, which they were trying to emulate. Pairing this with more powerful output transformers gave that warm overdrive that started the British invasion.

Seymour Duncan Convertible Head

The Seymour Duncan Convertible (see Figure 3.11) is an amp you don't hear much about, but it is an outstanding example of a true tone monster! When designing this amp, Seymour Duncan was ahead of his time with the idea of changing tubes for various tones without having to rebias the amp each time—something that THD hit on more than a decade later. The idea was that you could take one of several preamp cards, each with a mounted tube, and install them in the amp through a top-access door. You get anywhere from a nice bell tone Fender Twin to an overdrive that would rival Boogie. Don't take my word for it—just ask Jeff Beck. He still uses his Convertible.

Figure 3.11 Seymour Duncan Convertible.

The flexibility of the amp and its tone made it a treasure for studio recording. But the great feature about the amp was the built-in attenuator, in which you could go from 5 watts to 100 watts by turning a dial—very innovative for the time.

Industrial Rock 120 Combo/Overdrive 15 Head

These amps are a true hybrid between a Marshall and a Fender. But the overdrive channel really shines on its own. It reminds me of the Fender Prosonic series with the lush distortion and overtones.

What is really cool is the design. The tubes, transformers, and capacitors all cleverly reside behind 1/4-inch glass, so you can experience the mesmerizing glow of electronics at work. As an added bonus, the Rock 120 (see Figure 3.12) is tour-ready, boasting a set of large, riveted, zinc-coated handles with grips on both sides of the case, as well as four caster wheels for easy transport. Electronically, the amp features 120 watts, two channels (Classic and Heavy), point-to-point hand wiring, and an open-back cabinet fitted with two 12-inch Celestion 80s. Four premium 12AX7s, four EL34s, one 12AT7 for reverb, and a solid-state rectifier tube power the amp itself. The Overdrive 15 (see Figure 3.13) has three 12AX7 Pre Amp Tubes and two 6V6 Power Tubes. This is great for the studio. And don't let the 15 watts fool you—this baby can crank! Plus, the people at Industrial (www.industrialamps.com) are wonderful to deal with as well.

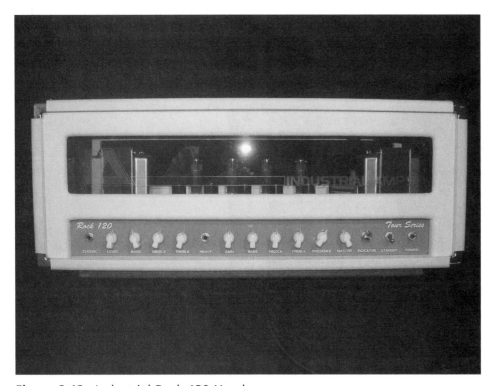

Figure 3.12 Industrial Rock 120 Head.

Fender Super Reverb

Super mojo is all that comes to mind. There is a reason why Stevie Ray Vaughan played Fender Super Reverb amps (see Figure 3.14) with such dedication. Super sound pushed at loud volumes reaches celestial tone heaven! Those 10-inch speakers are magic and break up nicely, delivering a blues punch. I turn to this amp quite often in the studio for both clean and brown tones. Try a 6-string semihollow electric through it, and you'll be in REM territory—or a 12-string at lower volumes, and you'll be reaching for the early '60s Rickenbacker tones. The best, of course, is taking out the Strat and ripping some real Hendrix blues licks through that famous Ibanez Tube Screamer or Dunlop wah. This a true tone amp. For those of you who haven't ever tried it, please do yourself a favor, get to your local vintage music store, and try one out.

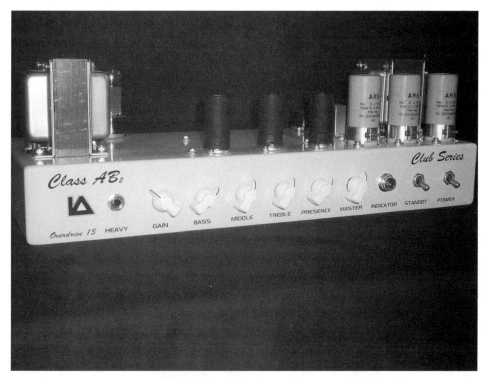

Figure 3.13   Overdrive 15 Head.

Figure 3.14   Fender Super Reverb.

Sovtek Tube Midget 50H

How can you dislike an amp made from old Soviet tank parts (see Figure 3.15)? But really, this amp can tear the paint off of most so-called high-gain amps today without breaking a sweat. The distinct beefy tone of these amps is a real treasure. This was the brainchild of none other than Mike Mathews of Electro-Harmonix. He figured the Soviets made such great tubes, why not have them make the whole amp? They were manufactured at factories in St. Petersburg, among other Russian cities. They had a high-quality sound with PCB construction, although some of them were point-to-point hand wired.

Figure 3.15   Sovtek Tube Midget 50H.

I run it through a 4 × 12 Legacy cabinet, Steve Vai signature series, and it sounds fat with a real punch of raw overdriven tone. With the master volume section, you can get the amp to desired overdriven tone without breaking the eardrums.

YBA-1 Traynor Bass Master

The YBA-1 Traynor Bass Master amp (see Figure 3.16) is often referred to as the "poor man's Plexi," which is not too far from the truth. The ability to jump two channels together as in the Marshall Plexis is very similar with dual pairs of inputs and dual volume controls. It is one of Canada's best exports from creators Jack Long, a music retailer, and Pete Traynor, a bass player.

Figure 3.16 Traynor YBA-1 Bass Master.

These amps are extremely well built to military specs and pioneered the first master volume in 1969, years before Marshall ever thought about it. I often use the Bass Master in stereo with a Marshall Plexi when recording lead parts, using the Framptone Amp Switcher (see Figure 3.17), giving the stereo image a deeper dimensional tone.

Figure 3.17 Framptone Amp Switcher.

The transformers alone are quite heavy and beefy. The tubes installed at the factory were two 6CA7s in the output stage, three 12AX7As in the preamp stage, and a 5AR4 rectifier tube. This is a real vintage beauty that offers clean tones for jazz and country.

Soldano Reverb-O-Sonic

Michael Soldano is in a league of his own when it comes to amp design. The man who took the Marshall further and deeper in tones showed the world how a boutique business can expand to international success. Soldano really took the classic principles and combined them with the modern world.

The Reverb-O-Sonic (see Figure 3.18) has 4 × 10 speakers that completely rock and are a perfect match with the overdrive circuitry. You can think of it as the updated Fender Super Reverb with drive for weeks! I used this amp with a Gibson ES 355 on the *Guitar Masters, Vol. 3 & 4: Les Paul Dedication* compilation I produced in memory of Les. It held up to the other guest guitarists I had on the CD, such as Steve Vai, Gary Hoey, Chris Poland, Frank Gambale, and Leslie West. How cool is an amp that actually goes up to 11 on the knobs! I love to record amps in stereo and often would juxtapose the Soldano on one side with the JTM 45 or the Traynor on the opposite side. It always makes it sound more organic, so there is a texture difference in the stereo field.

Figure 3.18 Soldano Reverb-O-Sonic.

Fat Tuned Guitars

One of the great never-ending quests that guitarists seek is the so-called fat tone from their trusty side arm. But the quagmire that so many players fall into is the bassy, muddy sound that fights against the kick drum and bass guitar frequencies.

There have been numerous guitar tracks that I've had to roll off the low midrange frequencies so they can actually fit into a mix. It may sound good in the room when wood shredding, but in the real world it just does not work alongside a band mix.

When adding those parameters with an eight-string electric guitar, you enter a new realm. Math metal bands, such as Meshuggah, Botch, and Revocation, have utilized the seven- and eight-string guitars very well without drowning out their bandmates. Those two extra low strings of F♯ and B really do some damage when used efficiently, making for a very effective tool! Here are some ideas on how to smash some heads without getting trapped with the mud in the mix.

Dealing with the Source

The first thing to do is get the right guitar tone from the source—that being from your guitar and amp. Don't be afraid to turn the knobs on your amp and the tone control on your guitar. I've recorded so many guitarists who just turn everything up to 10 and then are baffled that the tone is horrific. This is not brain surgery. For starters, it is best to stand or sit directly in front of your amp and play while tuning your tone in by adjusting the bass, treble, or presence controls or even your gain control on your amp. Maybe you need to turn the volume control down on your guitar or back off of your pedal devices. In short, there are so many different attributes that make up the sum of the tone.

Of course, another huge factor is the type of amp you are using—for example, tone from a 10-inch speaker will be different from that of a 12-inch speaker with an open-back cabinet as opposed to a closed back. Also consider the type of microphones and how they are positioned, because they play a role in the bass response. Using a Royer 121 figure-eight ribbon mic will be inherently different from using a Sennheiser 421 full-bodied cardioid pattern microphone, which has a five-position bass control.

Also many of today's mic preamps are equipped with EQs, such as the Universal Audio 610 and BAE 1073MPF. As you are recording, you can tweak your tone with the onboard EQ and really hone in on your sound. These are the elements that you have to contemplate when first recording the tracks, so you can eliminate possible bass frequency problems later in the mix.

Dealing with a Recorded Tone

So what happens when you are set up with your tone and you start to record and then realize that you are doing the mud tub tone? You get in tune with your parametric equalizers that allow you to select which frequency to adjust. Listen, it's not the end of the world that the tone you worked so hard to get is not right in the mix. As guitarists, we have all been there and have dealt with it.

One of my favorite EQs is the vintage Trident CB9066, an incredible transparent and musical tool. Malcolm Toft, the audio designer of Trident recording consoles, has not yet reissued this model or a compatible plug-in, but you never know. This EQ is extremely simple to use and does not have unnecessary bells and whistles. But the crème de la crème of EQs is, without a doubt, the reissued classic Pultec model EQP-1A3 by Pulse Technologies, by the genius of Steve Jackson.

Mr. Jackson, with a Ph.D. in electrical engineering, painstakingly created an incredible replica of the most prized EQ program equalizer from the 1950s. This device surgically removes every pesky low muddy frequency created from those eight-string guitars without disturbing the tone and effortlessly molds the guitar into the mix like a glove.

The EQP-1A3 provides a wide range of equalization curves, which makes it very easy to boost either very low- or very high-frequency notes without muddying up the middle register frequencies, and continuously variable controls that enable changing the amount of equalization on sustained tones without steps in level or noise. All controls are clickless, and a key permits cutting the equalizer in and out on cue. Pulse Technologies even goes to the extent of using new old stock tubes to stay true to the original specs.

We can't mention EQs without talking about Rupert Neve. I found the Rupert Neve Designs Portico 5033 five-band EQ to be a must-have for surgical equalizing. The 5033 is very flexible without being generic and without losing the Neve sound.

I know what you're thinking: Who has the cash for all of this expensive gear? I hear ya. I feel the pain as well! So for an inexpensive alternative, I recommend the Orban 622B, which houses two parametric EQs. It works fantastic on drums as well and can really tune in guitar frequencies, with four bands, each with tuning and bandwidth control, true parametric operation. You can buy these on eBay for $300, which is a great deal!

Now if you're an old analog dawg like myself, and you still use a mixing console, you know the natural thing to do is use the EQs already embedded on the board. So that is my first go-to, because that's where the audio signal is going through in my case. I have a vintage Trident recording console, so I use the onboard EQs to carve those tones for guitars.

In Practice

When I was producing the release *Fretworx*, I was up against some guitar tracks sent via email and discovered that the tracks had a muddy tone. In fact, the articulation of the guitar notes seemed to disappear within the mix, and they were drowned out by the frequencies of the bass guitar and kick drum. I found that compressing the track through the Urei LA-4 tightened the tone. But I still needed to cut some of that low-mid frequency and boost the high-mids, so I daisy-chained the signal out of the LA-4 through the Trident CB9066 Parametric EQ, which took the output of the EQ back into the return of the guitar channel. It worked perfectly in the mix and highlighted the finger articulation of the guitar without stepping all over the other instruments.

For another song, I ran the guitar through the Universal Audio LA-610, getting the best of both worlds: the high and low shelving EQ and the LA-2A-style T4 Opto-Compressor section.

When I was tracking and mixing Randy Covens's recent solo album, *Nu School*, I found the Portico 5033 five-band EQ and the Trident CB9066 to be lifesavers. Because Randy is a virtuoso bass player, both piccolo bass as well as regular bass, he played many of the melody lines, so there had to be a lot of separation of frequencies in the mixes. Add to this the huge sound of Leslie West—I really had to be on my toes to make sure everyone had clarity in the mix. I would bring Randy's bass up on one of the channels on the Trident mixer and use the insert points for the CB9066 or the Neve and then compress the heck out of the signal through the Universal Audio 1176 or the Purple Audio MC77. Worked like a charm!

I always tell musicians to trust their ears. Ears don't lie. If the mix sounds wrong, then 99 percent of the time it is wrong. Boosting the levels of instruments to try to compensate will just make a bad mix louder, and you'll find that all of your faders are pegged to the top without any headroom to move. The best solution is use a program equalizer that will blend the guitar perfectly within the mix. A little goes a long way; for example, a small boost at 3.3k or a cut at 300 Hz will be very effective. Don't be afraid to use the knobs—that's why Rupert Neve, Malcolm Toft, and Bob Orban engineered them!

Building a Guitar Recording Room

If you've been down this road before, or you are thinking about creating the perfect recording space, I've got some helpful step-by-step tips to make your space work for you.

First, if you browse your local bookstore, you will find that there are a plethora of books on the subject, containing numerous opinions on what issues to prioritize first. The considerations are endless, from studio size to acoustical treatment to wall panels and absorbers to diffusers, spacing of glass, sound reinforced doors, floating walls, ceilings, and floors to blah, blah, blah. But as my friends in New York say, "Not for nothin', what about the *electrical*?"

No matter how much money you spend on your design, whether it is a large professional studio or a small 8 × 8 room, do not overlook the importance of setting up the receptacles and lights first and foremost, before the wall goes up. Believe me. I learned this the hard way when I built my first studio. The wrong electrical setup can cause an irritating persistent hum that courses through the board and ultimately to your recordings. I ask you, what good is using an SSL, a Neve, or even a Trident recording console when the sound quality is stifled?

Ground loops are the most common problem in home studios, as is that nasty light noise that feeds itself from wall dimmers. Having built a number of studios and grappled with this common problem with grounding noise, I decided to help a colleague build a recording studio in an empty industrial building in Nevada over the summer. This time, I took a journal and a digital camera to record the process, which I will share with you here.

Get Clean Electricity

Ground loops, a major cause of hum in audio and video systems, are created by improperly designed or improperly installed equipment. They also present an electric shock hazard, which we guitarists know all too well. Have you ever played through an old Fender amp when the ground switch on the back is accidentally turned off? You touch the guitar strings and a piece of metal on the amp and *zap*! Thank you very much for that! Well, same idea. For instance, if two pieces of audio equipment are plugged into different power outlets, there will often be a difference in their respective ground potentials. If a signal is passed from one to the other via an audio connection with the ground wire intact, this potential difference will cause a current through the cables, generating an audible buzz. You get this with certain keyboard workstations as well, so use a ground lifter—that little orange plug that has no ground prong on the end. Use it on everything, so as to dodge that surprising shock, especially if you are ground lifting audio equipment.

The best way to eliminate this problem is to use ground-isolated reciprocals (orange outlets—see Figure 3.19). I highly recommend that you use a licensed electrician to install them. It won't be cheap, but your recordings depend on it. You should only use orange receptacles for your studio equipment to ensure no unwanted hums. Otherwise, there's a good chance of getting feedback noise in your mixes from that microwave or mini refrigerator. I have worked in studios where a sudden surge from the microwave caused this crazy buzzing sound in the audio during a session. It always struck me as funny when guys worried about the microphone placement but never addressed obvious electrical hums buzzing all around their studios.

Figure 3.19 Orange outlets.

Lighting

It's now time to address the lighting issues. If you are like many musicians who like to record under dim lights, you'll need to invest in what is called an *incandescent lighting control*. Incandescent lighting is used extensively in residential, theatrical, institutional, commercial, and industrial installations. Dimmers are continuously adjustable transformers that regulate light intensity by controlling the voltage applied to the lamps. Basically, an incandescent lighting control offers a smooth performance with no audio or video interference. If you use a cheap $3 dimmer from Home Depot, as you dim the lights there will be horrible noise interference in the audio. Superior Electric makes a wall dimmer box called the Powerstat. Professional recording studios around the world house several of these units in their facilities (see Figure 3.20).

Figure 3.20 Powerstat dimmer.

Building the Wall

On this particular project we were dealing with one large open space, from which we needed to create a control room and a separate live room. We had to figure a creative and affordable way of dividing the space, which had 13-foot ceilings. So I started by breaking the room into two halves, and at the narrowest point between walls, I built an 8-foot wall. First I framed it out with two-by-sixes at a height of 8 feet (see Figure 3.21). Once it was framed out, I mounted the Powerstat wall box in the control room and the orange receptacles in both the live room and the control room.

We had brought in a double-paned 4 × 6-foot window for the control room, to look out into the live room. We placed it within the wall frame (see Figure 3.22). Then our trusty electrician came in and wired everything back to the box: outlets, dimmer, and track lights.

Now it was time to finish the wall. To contain the noise factor, we used mounting sound board, which you can find at Home Depot or Lowe's, and nailed it directly onto the frame. Once the frame was completely covered, we added knotty pine wood paneling (see Figure 3.23) to add warmth to the space. After that we had to address the 5 feet of space between the frame and ceiling. I wanted something that would be more flexible and lighter, so we didn't have to build another heavy wall. So I framed it with two-by-fours and used an acoustical treatment made by the company Acoustical Solutions (see Figure 3.24). The product is called AlphaSorb Barrier

Figure 3.21   Framed-out wall.

Figure 3.22   Window.

Figure 3.23   Insulation and pine panels.

Figure 3.24 Acoustical treatment.

Fabric Wrapped Wall Panels, consisting of AudioSeal Sound Barrier with the addition of the sound barrier septum. These panels offer an outstanding STC rating of 29 combined with an NRC rating of 0.85 to 1.05. This is a very good bang for the buck. Plus you can get the panels custom-made to any size. The fabric wraps one-inch rigid fiberglass with a sheet of sound barrier vinyl in between. We used a nail gun and got the panels up quickly.

As for the door that fits between the live room and the studio, we used a heavy single-swing 3 × 7-foot acoustical door fitted with a small window purchased from Acoustical Solutions. The door is available with STC (Sound Transmission Classification) ratings from STC 41 up to STC 57. What's great about Acoustical Solutions is that they also make custom doors, as well as over-sized, undersized, double doors, swinging doors, tandem doors, and doors with or without windows (see Figure 3.25).

You will also need a reliable doorjamb seal that fits above the door to the wall. Acoustical Solutions makes an acoustical seal, which features a unique Compress-o-Matic design with a sound-absorbing neoprene rubber gasket that compresses to form a tight seal as the door is closed. The doorjamb seals include adjusting screws for field correction of irregular clearances that might otherwise compromise the sound performance. This ensures a tight seal for the door, and the adjust feature is useful in future adjustments.

Control Room to Major Tom

This is the room where everything goes down. This is where you'll live, both to track and mix, so it's got to be right. In the control room area we were dealing with cement walls. So I built a floating wall system framed with two-by-fours, making sure to angle all of the corners. The frames were then fastened with cement wall screws at strategic places to hold everything tightly in place (see Figure 3.26).

I then took more panels of the AlphaSorb Barrier Fabric Wrapped Wall Panels and placed them on the outside frame side by side and screwed the panels in place. This designated wall was

Figure 3.25   Acoustical door.

Figure 3.26   Wall treatment.

where we placed the Trident mixing console (see Figure 3.27). Because we were dealing with a space with high ceilings and a lot of cement, we also hung a few heavy-duty oriental rugs on the back wall to absorb some of the reflection from the monitors and slap back from side to side.

One of the largest undertakings was dealing with the 13-foot industrial ceiling, with exposed beams and insulation. We wanted to leave the openness of the space, but we also needed to control the sound for mixing. I designed a large angled sound reflector (8 × 8 feet) that would be installed above the mixing console. I started out by building a standalone frame using two-by-fours. I then secured the top of the hanging frame to the wood beams on the ceiling and the

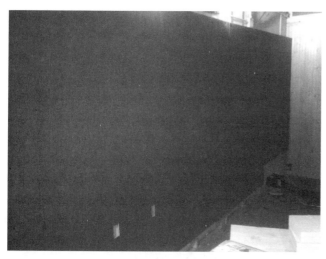

Figure 3.27   Finished wall treatment.

bottom of the frame to the cement wall at a 90-degree angle (see Figure 3.28). Because of the 13-foot ceiling it was a bit tricky, but with the help of a 12-foot ladder, a power miter saw, and cement screws, I got the frame secured.

Figure 3.28   Ceiling baffle frame.

The next issue to tackle was what material to use to cover the frame. I decided to cover the frame with a quarter inch of plywood with the pine furring across in rows, to ensure evenness. Once the basic framing of the reflector was done (see Figure 3.29), I chose two sheets of composite board measuring 4 × 8 feet, which I cut into four quarters each and glued four Auralex 2 × 2-foot squares to each of the panels. This made it lot easier to lift them up to the frame and fasten. For the top pieces, we had to use a pulley device so we could hold them in place while we screwed the panels in place. The Auralex foam had to be pulled back a few inches so we could place the screws directly through the plywood to the frame, so as not to mess up the look of the foam (see Figure 3.30).

Figure 3.29 Ceiling baffle board.

Figure 3.30 Finished ceiling baffle.

Now there was a question of the back wall. This was made of wood, and it was a straight shot up to the ceiling. As I mentioned earlier, we hung two rugs on the back wall, but they were only 5 × 7 feet each. So I fabricated diamond-shaped wall treatments to be hung in strategic places in the room. I used 12 two-by-threes and three sheets of 4 × 8-foot Luan board. What is Luan? It's a quarter-inch sheet of plywood veneer board, the same material usually used as an interior wall or floor of a house. I took four two-by-twos and framed the two-by-threes around to fit and placed the Luan plywood underneath as a base. I made three of these traps, placing two on the back wall about 9 feet up, spaced about 7 feet apart, and hung the last one on the perpendicular wall on the left, above the AlphaSorb Barrier Fabric Wrapped Wall Panels. Aesthetically they looked great and worked perfectly at absorbing sound, so we built three more of these traps and placed them in the live room as well.

Conclusion

I must say, every time I embark on such a journey, the studio space I am working with has never been the same space, size, or dimensions. I learn so much about the way sound works within its confinements and how it travels. If you would like to delve further into building your own space, some good reference books to check out are *Sound Studio Construction on a Budget* (McGraw-Hill, 1996) by F. Alton Everest and *Home Recording Studio: Build It Like the Pros* (Course Technology PTR, 2006) by Rod Gervais.

What I've learned through trial and error is no matter what the dimensions of your studio, the main thing is that the space is comfortable and conducive to your needs. Also, immediately address any harsh or bad reflected areas in the room. I've been in studio control rooms where I had no idea how the engineer could mix, given the many sorts of crazy reflections and structural interferences scattered around the room.

This brings me back to those early days of recording, as a solo artist for Instinct Records, when they sent me to London to record my first album. The producer had the most unusual recording studio nestled in the attic of an old brownstone. The space was crammed, and the ceilings were low. I could barely stand up straight, so I did all of my recordings sitting down in a room that was also the control room where the producer sat. It was like being in a tree fort with low-hanging eaves and a slanted window that overlooked the smokestacks atop roofs down the street. But what went through my mind the whole time was, "How in the world can anyone mix in a room like this?" I didn't stay there for the mixes, but when we heard the final production they were fantastic! In fact, the album went on to chart top 10 at Radio and top 40 on Billboard. Perhaps the saving grace was that the producer recorded the CD on his Otari 90 24-track analog machine through a Neve console.

At the end of the day, I really believe it's your ears that produce the best sound, because the best of them can mix a great record in an empty swimming pool. So don't get trapped by all of these high-end pro audio sites trying to sell you $6,000 control windows, because it's not what you spend—it's how you use it!

4 In the Mix with Great Dynamics, Mic Pres, and Effects Processors

I t's the age-old question of how to keep your guitar in the mix without losing the integrity of the tone. Engineers have been grappling with this for years to have it stand tall in the saddle without dominating everything else. This is why the guitar was instinctively the best candidate to amplify, because acoustically the guitar has a very soft and delicate sound. Thanks to Seth Lover and our dear departed friend Les Paul for the invention of guitar pickups and amplification, the guitar became the aggressive beast we've come to know and love, not to mention the backbone of rock-n-roll.

Eventide Harmonizer H3000

The Eventide Harmonizer H3000 (see Figure 4.1) is an old-school effects processor that is a true workhorse for guitar effects. There are so many classic sounds in this unit. My particular favorite patches are H949 (one output is a straight delay and the other is pitch-shifted delay), Micropitch-shift (perfect effect to fatten up a sound—great on bass), Scary Movie (it's a reverse-shift sound creating evil voices—awesome on guitar), Canyon (huge-sounding reverb with an echo effect—awesome for solos), Analog Delays (filtered delays with a little swept effect), and Dual H910s (this emulates two 910 units together, with left and right sides processed separately). When this processor was first released, it was very advanced and cutting edge. Today, it stands as a top guitar processor. It is also very easy to edit with the soft key function below the LED window. Every guitarist should have one.

Eventide Harmonizer GTR 4000

A great effects processor developed specifically for guitar players, this Eventide has so many useful presets from the factory that can be easily tweaked and edited. There are some really fun artist patches, such as "Kill the Guy" and "Little Man" under the Steve Vai bank and "Gorgeous Delay" and "Satchelope Filter" under the Joe Satriani presets.

What's cool is that the 4000 series has a graphical editor to allow users to really construct their sound. This makes the 4000 so versatile, because the effects are made up of smaller building blocks referred to as *modules*. It's extremely useful and flexible because you can use these modules not only on your input signal, but also elsewhere in the signal chain. For example, you could

Figure 4.1   Eventide Harmonizer H3000 and Eventide Harmonizer GTR 4000.

use a flange on the output of a reverb. For guitar nuts like us, this is such a cool feature because we always like to experiment with our sound.

Lexicon PCM 70

We all know how wonderful the Lexicon reverb sounds, and this unit lives up to that, even though it is an old-school processor (see Figure 4.2). Take, for instance, the Concert Wave preset. It really responds well to clean and bright sources like that spanking Strat sound or even a nice hollow-body clean tone. The Six Across preset is a favorite because it contains six voices that are all filtered to different bandwidths and panned to different locations in the stereo field. Another nice preset is the Soft Echoes, which I usually use on acoustic guitars. It contains a reverb effect, which starts off with four discrete predelay echoes. Turning the soft knob control lengthens the RT times and ultimately makes the ambience brighter. It also has multieffects, such as the Flange O Echo, Voice Combo, and Echorus—all very nice-sounding patches.

Figure 4.2   Eventide Eclipse and Lexicon PCM 70.

Eventide Eclipse

Yeah, I know—another Eventide product. But they are an outstanding company for guitar processors. This is a modern-day Ultra-Harmonizer, with some great new presets and some classic updated sounds, as well as combination sounds such as PitchModTrem, Ringdelays, LofoFilter +Pong, and Swampy Guitar. What is super awesome is the Tempo Tap button, which allows you to get the right BPM on the fly. It's very user friendly and intuitive. So when you load a program, all of the important parameters are located under the Hot Keys button.

Programs are made up of an effect's blocks, which you can access through the Parameters button. Each effects block runs the Eclipse's set of algorithms. This is the building block of the unit and is very easy to understand when you dig into the effects processor. When I was recording Leslie West, he really liked the program PanVerbEcho, so I would print the effect alone on another track so we could use it in the mix.

Electro-Harmonix NY-2A Stereo Limiter

What kind of optical compressor can be so flexible that it allows the user to adjust the actual light source from incandescent, to LED, to electroluminescent with a rotary knob? Welcome to the world of the NY-2A Limiter by Electro-Harmonix (see Figure 4.3). The incandescent lamp has the slowest attack time, with a little kink in its response. The LED lamp has a much faster attack time and a much faster frequency response. The electroluminescent (EL) lamp has the most interesting reaction to frequencies; it actually changes colors with each frequency range. So the EL lamp produces less light at low frequencies, more in the middle, and much much more at high frequencies. There is also a squash switch that will act as a high-frequency shelving for the EL lamp. How does it sound? Fantastic for guitars! You can do a lot of experimenting with the unit on different guitar parts, with the flexibility of the settings. Again the controls are very simple, with Pre-Gain, Compress, and Post-Gain knobs, so a lot of the compression will depend on your input level.

Figure 4.3 Electro-Harmonix NY-2A.

Rupert Neve 5043 Compressor-Limiter

The Rupert Neve 5043 (see Figure 4.4) is a fantastic stereo buss compressor, which can also be used as two independent compressor-limiters (channels A and B). This type of compressor technology uses a VCA, or voltage-controlled amplifier. There are many types of voltage controls, including the use of tubes, discrete and integrated solid-state circuits, and naturally nonlinear devices, each one having its own sonic character. This has a very accurate low-noise, low-distortion VCA—in

Figure 4.4 Rupert Neve 5043.

other words, very transparent. But with that said, it does have that Neve sound without being too obtrusive. Great for rock music of all types, it has such a beautiful full sound that really makes the guitar pop out of the track. It also can add a gain from –6 dB to 20 dB and has a ratio from 1:1 all the way to 40:1. This compressor is so musical and loves guitars of all sorts. I used this quite a lot on producing the *Guitar Masters, Volume 3 & 4: Les Paul Dedication*—everything from bass to stereo buss compressor from the mix to crunch guitars.

BAE 1073 Mic Pre

This is a sweet-sounding mic pre based on the classic Neve 1073 (see Figure 4.5). It uses the same 283 card and transformers as the original for the fraction of the cost. For those of you who are doing digital recording only, this is a must-have mic pre for guitar! It adds warmth to the guitar tone and fattens up the overall sound. It has a very present tone, so you really hear the attack of the pick and fingers on the fretboard without having to compress. It adds subharmonics to the bottom end, making it feel large without the mud, and it adds silkiness to the high frequencies, giving it a sheen. It has a red gain knob and a gray output. Every click on the gain knob is a 5-dB increment, so you can always adjust the output level to get in between the 5-dB steps. With its large headroom, it is an excellent choice for the low-output ribbon microphones.

Figure 4.5 BAE 1073.

Trident Dual Limiter-Compressor CB9146

This is probably one of the most transparent compressors I've ever used. I don't want a compressor to stamp a color or sound onto my guitars. I just want to control uneven levels and retain the natural tone of the guitar. As with the 1176, this uses the FET technology, and it's very easy to use with the color-coded knobs. However, the Trident has attack and release controls, which the 1176 lacks. In fact, the Trident (see Figure 4.6) has a large variety of control combinations that can achieve different compression. It is great on a buss as well for drums or guitars, leaving the natural characteristics of the source tone. These are real classic limiters dating back to the '70s,

Figure 4.6 Trident Dual Limiter.

originally designed to have a source apparent volume to be louder. In fact, you couldn't get breathing effect if you tried. This compressor is so musical and highly recommended.

Universal Audio 1176

Technically, the Universal Audio 1176 (see Figure 4.7) is a gain-limiting amplifier using the FET technology. So what's an FET? The acronym stands for *field effect transistor*, which is used as a voltage-controlled variable resistor shunt. Using the FET enables large amounts of limiting without getting increased distortion. In other words, it sounds dope! It's very easy to use—by controlling the input, you are controlling the compression along with the compression ratio from 4:1 to 20:1. It sounds fantastic on so many things, from acoustic guitars to bass guitars and even percussions, such as a snare drum.

Figure 4.7 Universal Audio 1176.

When producing bass virtuoso Randy Coven's CD *Nu School*, I used this on his bass all the time, because it reacted well to his tone and style of playing, on both the five-string and piccolo bass. It also worked perfectly when used on a mono drum room mic with all of the buttons in. It gave that huge, overcompressed sound. I would blend the track into the drum mix to give some more ambience.

JDK R20 Channel Mic Pre

I love a mic preamp with a VU meter so you know what kind of input/output is happening. The JDK R20 (see Figure 4.8) is a very well-made mic pre. And how can you go wrong with the design team of API behind it? With the pad switch attenuating the microphone signal by 20 dB (the instrument signal by 10 dB) and the 54 dB of gain, this is a good choice for most microphones. Though some would say it's not enough gain for a ribbon mic, I've never had a problem miking a cabinet. It has a nice warm, transparent sound that leaves the precious guitar tone intact.

Figure 4.8   JDK R20 mic pre.

It's extremely easy to use—there is just a gain knob that determines your input/output signal. It has a smooth sound that captures the accurate guitar tone as you hear it in the room. This is a very different type of mic pre from the BAE 1073 because it is a transformerless mic preamp, which means the gain stage is directly wired as opposed to running through a transformer, common in classic mic pres. It's very affordable and a fine choice for all types of guitars.

Useful Effects Pedals

We all know how guitarists love pedal effects. There's no greater feeling than absorbing the sound from your guitar through a ring modulator, flanger, wah, and so on, so you get goose bumps from those awesomely strange and haunting sounds. Today, it seems as if every tone junkie is building some sort of effect stompbox in his basement. These odd and beautiful boxes are as personal to guitarists as their guitars themselves. Because after all, these are a part of our tone—an extension of our own expression and the actual notes that come from our fingers spanning the fretboard.

Snarling Dogs Mold Spore Wah

The Snarling Dogs Mold Spore (see Figure 4.9) is a monster wah with that *Star Trek* mold spore sound! It has great control as a wah pedal, better than the run-of-the-mill Dunlop pedals, which results in more expression. The wah has three basic sounds: White Room (thick and creamy), Voodoo (midrange growl), and Shaft (sharp and funky). The mold spore part of the wah is a secret weapon that will knock you out. It is a ring modulator on steroids. There is a freakwincy tone that can be set with a chickenhead knob on the side of the pedal, and if used with the wah turned on, you have a filter depending on where the wah is set. I have used this countless times when recording the soundtrack band Asphalt Jungle; it's an excellent choice for electronica music. It has become my main wah pedal because of its flexibility on different styles of music, from rock to funk to jazz.

Electro-Harmonix Deluxe Memory Man

I remember when they introduced the Electro-Harmonix Deluxe Memory Man pedals (see Figure 4.10). Back in the day growing up in NYC, I used to go down to 48th Street and window-shop at all of the guitar stores. There used be an Electro-Harmonix demo store a couple doors down from Manny's, on the other side of the theater. It was a blast to go there and test out the

Figure 4.9   Snarling Dogs Mold Spore.

Figure 4.10   Deluxe Memory Man.

entire pedal line. I remember they had different stations set up with guitars, and you could test various pedals through amps. Of course, one of the pedal highlights was the Memory Man, a cool analog delay. The surge of electronic music in the '90s brought these pedals back to the foreground—in particular, the overly popular Chemical Brothers. In 1997, when they came out with their big hit "Block Rockin' Beats," I knew I recognized that crazy sound effect—it was none other than the Memory Man! Crank those feedback and delay controls, and you get the unforgettable effect. Well done!

Boss Super Octave OC-3

The Boss Super Octave OC-3 (see Figure 4.11) is great-sounding octave divider. The three modes provided are the polyphonic octave, a drive mode with distortion, and the original OC-2 mode. Again, when I was producing the Randy Coven CD, I put him through this effect on more than one occasion, and the effect was stunning. The drive mode with distortion is so cool, and you can control the distortion level. It is great on bass solos and when adding different textures in a track. Try using it on a lower-register riff part and then double-tracking it on the higher register of the guitar—really fat! Try a clean-sounding guitar—say, an ES 335—play some jazz riffs, and put the

Figure 4.11 Boss Super Octave OC-3.

mix lower for the effect, and you will get a very nice effect in the track. The poly octave effect adjusts to play within a specific note range—very handy when tracking single parts.

Keeley Time Machine Boost Pedal

I often use the Keeley Time Machine Boost pedal (see Figure 4.12) on my Marshall Plexi 100-watt head through a 4 × 12 cabinet. It produces a terrific response to the tubes and has three distinct era sounds. There are two channels labeled Vintage (1966 and 1971 settings) and the modern, which has a warp mode setting. The modern side uses a +23-dB gain dual JFET, which gets into the territory of Mesa Boogie in terms of ultimate overdrive tone machine. What's nice about this pedal is that there is very little coloration to your guitar tone except giving you boost/saturation to your amp tone. I also put it through a Marshall JTM45, which saturates the tone further but still keeps the natural sound of the amp.

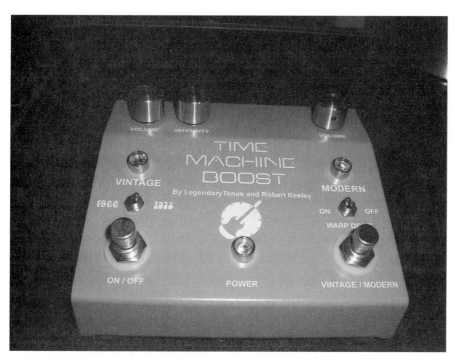

Figure 4.12   Time Machine Boost.

Keeley Ibanez Tube Screamer TS808

This is the legendary 808 pedal, but modified by Keeley for outstanding performance (see Figure 4.13). Basically it has the new JRC chip installed in it, as well as the increase of the gain range, meaning it gets cleaner and more distorted through the range of the drive control. Keeley also addresses the limited bass response that cuts so much of the huge midrange bump in the sound. And they modified the tone control, enabling the user to get more bass frequency response.

Aside from all the technical stuff, just plug it in an old Fender Super Reverb and listen to that sweet tone and how improved it sounds from the original. When recording Leslie West, I put

Figure 4.13 Tube Screamer.

him through the Marshall JCM800 with this pedal, and it was overdrive heaven, catching all of those pinch harmonics.

Dunlop Uni-Vibe

Can you say Robin Trower, *Bridge of Sighs*? The Dunlop Uni-Vibe (see Figure 4.14) is a great reissue of the original, which always had a lot of electrical issues back in the day. It's not just a cheap chorus pedal—it is so much more! The sound has an incredible rotary/Leslie cabinet–sounding pedal, boasting hand-matched photoresistors with a long-life incandescent lamp. This is a true Hendrix machine, right from the stages of Woodstock!

I love putting a clean-sounding semihollow-body guitar through it and hearing the distinctiveness of each string in a chord go from one side of the stereo field to the other. When I was producing the track "Tarquinius Maximus" for the compilation *Guitar Masters Vol. 3 & 4: Les Paul Dedication*, I used it on the clean rhythm tracks, and Chris Poland took a solo using this sound as well. Pure mojo!

Electro-Harmonix Micro Synth

This is a really sick over-the-top pedal by the effects guru himself, Mike Mathews. It's a very cool effect, and if you're like me, you'd rather play the synth sounds through your guitar than through

Figure 4.14 Dunlop Uni-Vibe.

a keyboard. You can get everything from the classic Moog sounds to new experimental sounds. The pedal has a two-pole analog resonant filter, a four-voice mixer section (suboctave, original, octave up, and square wave), a square wave voice that can be used as a distortion tone, and start/stop filter frequency sliders with adjustable rate for full control over the filter's sweep direction and speed. You can also adjust the attack time control for fading in notes. It's great for experimental electronica music—I have used it on a number of drum and bass tracks I produced on the Asphalt Jungle CD, *Junglization*. This is a fun pedal for a guitar to dig into and get those old analog synth sounds.

Slick EQ Units

Equalization is a really important factor in recording. It can be used as an effect or as a correction tool in the mix. I love EQ and have become a junkie for its tone pleasures! For certain types of music, such as electronic, you can really twist and curve guitar tones into spiral contortions that squeeze your eardrums dry! Take the classic Urei Little Dipper, which has a variable high-pass and low-pass filter with excellent band restriction. It was originally used by the film industry and broadcast, but when used on a musical source such as a guitar, it can do radical phase frequency shifts. However you use EQs, don't be afraid to really dig in deep and spin those knobs—after all, that's why EQ was made!

JDK R24 Dual Channel 4-Band EQ

The JDK R24 (see Figure 4.15) is a great, flexible EQ that has an array of applications for recording. You can warm up a guitar sound or notch out certain frequencies with ease. This was modeled after the classic APSI model 562 EQ, and each band offers continuously variable control of frequency and gain, using separate knobs. It has 12 dB of boost/cut per band, and all four bands are peak/dipping parametric configuration with a high headroom +24 dB clip level. The great thing is that this EQ has a very transparent sound, which is perfect for guitar tracks,

Figure 4.15   JDK R24 EQ.

so the original guitar tone is not altered. You can even put it across a mix buss because they come in pairs. I put it across a guitar stereo mix, and once I placed it into the whole mix, the guitars popped right out of the speakers. Remember that with EQ, a little goes a long way, so experiment all you want before the final mix.

Pulse Techniques EQP-1A3

The Pulse EQP-1A3 (see Figure 4.16) sounds fantastic. I put a couple of mono guitar tracks through it and put it to the test. First I ran an aggressive bass part by Billy Sheehan, and I have to say it really gave it a full spectrum of sound, without the mud. It let me home into the low-mids, which gave the bass true detail as well as sharpened up the notes in the mix. On Billy's solo part, it worked beautifully by letting me attenuate the higher mid frequencies to showcase his solo.

Figure 4.16   Pulse EQP-1A3.

I also put a Frank Gambale solo I recorded through the EQP-1A3 with pleasing results. The tubes really gave warmth to the aggressively distorted guitar tone, without taking away from their signature sounds. Having the bandwidth from sharp to broad is a great asset to carve in the sound. I found myself not even looking at the unit, but just slowly dialing in the tone with my head between the monitors, stopping when I hit the mark! The ears don't lie, and the EQP-1A3 is a great tool for those who still believe that sound matters.

Trident Parametric EQ CB9066

The Trident Parametric EQ CB9066 (see Figure 4.17) is my go-to EQ for guitars and bass. It is probably the most transparent parametric EQ I have ever heard. Like all the classic Trident gear, the Parametric EQ consists of five color-coded section knobs. The blue knob controls the frequency (100 Hz to 400 Hz) and slope (0 dB to 22 dB); the gold knobs are the bandwidth pot, dB gain (–16 to +16), and frequency pot (60 Hz to 700 Hz); the black knobs control bandwidth pot, dB gain (–16 to +16), and frequency pot (600 Hz to 7 kHz); the red knobs control the bandwidth pot, dB gain (–16 to +16), and frequency pot (3.5 kHz to 14 kHz); and the green knobs control frequency (4 kHz to 15 kHz) and slope (0 dB to 22 dB).

Figure 4.17 Trident EQ.

All in all, it is a very intuitive unit and can easily be used to achieve some great sounds. This was my weapon of choice chained together with the 1176 for all of Randy Covens's sounds. I was able to carve out a nice tone for his bass solos and then squash the signal in the 1176 at a ratio 12:1.

Rupert Neve Portico 5033 5-Band EQ

I want to preface the following with the comment that there's no magic box; if there were, everybody would have bought one years ago, and there would be no need for any other device. Rupert Neve once said, "The problem with my EQs is that everyone uses them"—the point being that it is traditionally thought that EQ is used only seldom, and if there is need for EQ on a source, you should move the microphone and re-record the source instead of using EQ at all.

With that said, Neve EQs do rock, and the 5033 (see Figure 4.18) is no exception! The input and output transformers are custom designed by Neve, which is the real secret to all Neves. The EQ is based on his traditional curves, –/+12 dB input level adjustment, and it has that Neve sound; it's not as transparent as other EQs, but it still has the Neve hallmark sound. It is an incredible flexible EQ, and you can really dial a plethora of sounds from corrective EQ or use it as an effect.

Figure 4.18 Rupert Neve 5033.

Orban Parametric EQ Model 622B

The Orban EQ 622B (see Figure 4.19) is an awesome tool to have in your recording arsenal. It is a dual EQ that offers four bands, each with tuning and bandwidth control, true parametric operation: noninteracting control over all these equalization parameters, +16 dB to infinity equalization range, "Constant-Q" curves, each band tuning over 25:1 frequency range, and "Q" a variable between 0.29 and 3.2.

Figure 4.19 Orban EQ 622B.

So what does that mean? It means that it is one heck of an EQ. Originally these were designed for broadcast use, but they quickly became a studio favorite. I use the 622B a lot on drums and when I want to dial in the heavy guitar rhythm *a la* Pantera or Megadeth territory. The filters are well made, and notch filtering is achieved easily. By adjusting the MLF and MHF bands close together in frequency, you can achieve that old telephone or radio effect. You can also get the amp hum off of a track by using the narrowband-notching mode, which is very helpful when using those single coils or P90s in the studio.

Akai MFC42 Analog Filter Module

I really enjoy working with the Akai MFC42 (see Figure 4.20). I put some overdriven guitars through it for an electronic TV score I was working on for ABC-TV. The EQ features a stereo and a mono filter channel, which can be controlled independently, linked together, or inverted. Each channel is selectable between any one of four filter types: low pass, high pass, band pass, and notch. The stereo channel features dual two-pole or four-pole filters, and the mono channel has two-pole, four-pole, or eight-pole selectable filters (maximum combination is four two-pole filters total).

Figure 4.20 Akai MFC42.

The effects are dynamite: distortion with depth control, analog stereo phase shifter with speed and depth controls, and master EQ with separate low and high controls. These controls make it easy to get those sweeping filter effects on guitar tracks. What is extremely cool is that you can control the movement of each knob or button via MIDI recording to an external sequencer for complete automation. I used this quite a lot on the Asphalt Jungle recordings to get those huge filter sweeps on guitars.

Guitar Pickups

We can thank inventors such as Seth Lover for the creation of the double humbucker pickup, which fed our obsession for great tone through pickups. Gibson started the whole thing in 1936 with their electric guitar model ES 150, which became the landmark guitar of Charlie Christian. But Les Paul, the father of electric guitar, really came up with the genius idea of a solid-body guitar routed out for two pickups—can you say that it goes to 11? With the solid body, you could really crank it out and get that sweet tone. Who knew back then that this would influence the rock-n-roll guitar heroes of 20th century to swagger, spin, and smash their electric guitars on stage—and yes, we loved it!

Seymour Duncan Blackout Single AS-1

The Blackout Single AS-1 will kick your butt, if you dare! I've always been a double humbucker guy, particularly with Gibson guitars. But finally there is a pickup that has a hot output! It reminds me a little of the Eric Clapton preamp system, without the separate preamp. The AS-1 runs on an active circuitry and has a nine-volt battery. Run it through a high-distortion amp, and it really shines with saturation. I have an old Mesa Boogie 50-caliber amp head and ran it through a Carvin Legacy 4 × 12, and it sounded amazing! It retains the single-coil tone but with so much more output. This is the way a Strat should sound. And of course, when backed off on the volume on the guitar, the output cleans up. Just the way I like it—loud and proud, none of this antiquity stuff for me.

Seymour Duncan Pearly Gates SH-PG1 and TBPG-1

Do you like pinch harmonics and Billy Gibbons? Well, this is the pickup that gets it right on the money. It has beautiful tone for the taking. Think of a stock Gibson '59 humbucker with more output. You can really hear the fingers on the fretboard from this pickup. Years ago, I was recording a track for a film called *The Watcher* with Keanu Reeves, and they wanted a ZZ Top track for a scene. So I had an '83 Kramer Striker in my guitar arsenal loaded with Pearly Gates in the bridge position. I went into the studio and cut the "Tush" soundalike track and really nailed that Billy Gibbons tone, pinch harmonics and all. Needless to say, the producers loved the track, and it made the film. Thank God for those Pearly Gates!

Seymour Duncan Seth Lover Model SH-55

Who in the heck is Seth Lover? Well, let me drop some knowledge on you! While working at the Gibson factory in 1955, Seth Lover invented the humbucker picks, PAF (patent applied for). Before the humbucker invention, everyone was forced to deal with the inherent 60-cycle hum in single-coil pickups. Lover wired two coils electrically out of phase and with reversed magnetic polarities, which canceled the hum before it reached the amp, hence bucking that hum. It was one of the best inventions in history for the electric guitar! So Seymour Duncan and Seth Lover jointly designed this pickup, with a bit of a microphonic tone because the cover is not waxed potted. This is a very vintage-sounding pickup and great for a nice clean tone.

Fender Custom Shop Texas Special

Think of the late, great Stevie Ray Vaughan. This is the best replication for his tone, with a midrange chirp, crystal highs, and tight bass along with increased output. They use the alnico 5 magnets and enamel-coated magnet wire. The middle pickup is reverse wound/reverse polarity for hum canceling in positions 2 and 4. Excellent though a Marshall JMP series from the '70s, it can even nail the Ritchie Blackmore sound from those delicious Deep Purple days. It reacts great with pedals, especially boost pedals that give off a sweet saturation tone.

Fender Eric Clapton Noiseless System

Here is a very well-balanced set of pickups running on a nine-volt battery with a powerful active midboost (+25 dB) preamp and TBX circuits. It's very versatile, ranging from the crystal bright clean tones of Robert Cray to the massive overdriven tones of Kings X. The push/pull pot that boosts the midrange is quite handy when pushing the preamp and creates a distinct tone. But you will really feel the air move when you push it through a high-gain Marshall amp, such as the JCM2000. I had a purple Fender Jeff Beck Signature Strat once loaded with these pickups—the best of both artists—and it burned, as the Deep Purple song states!

Gibson Dirty Fingers

I remember when these pickups with attitude debuted more than 20 years ago. As the Gibson literature said back then, it was [t]he critical union between power and dirt"—and they weren't kidding. These guys shine on a Les Paul Custom and an ES 335. They have bark and a bite to them and a really nice high output for rock tones. But on the other hand, back off of the guitar volume, and you will hear a clear tone.

I've used these pickups on a Gibson ES 355 Lucille model through a Soldano Reverb O Sonic with 4×10s, and it absolutely screamed when I pushed the gain. And by the same token, it cleaned up very nicely when the gain was brought down, giving off a very bluesy tone.

Gibson Mini Humbucker

This is one of my favorite humbuckers of all time. It sounds fantastic. Don't let the "mini" in the name fool you—the Mini Humbucker is awesome, with tone for days! They first arrived on the scene featured in the 1969 Les Paul Deluxe guitar, the first Les Paul production in years. The pickups were also known as New York humbuckers. These pickups fit into the precarved P-90 pickup cavity using an adaptor ring developed by Gibson, which started the standardization of production for U.S.-built Gibsons.

The bridge position can crank it up and sounds best through a nice high-gain amp, pinch harmonics and all! The neck position has such a rich warmth to it for clean jazz tones and octaves. Just back off of the tone control in the neck position, and you'll swear you have an ES 335. When I was a solo artist on Instinct Records back in the day, I used this setup in a 1977 Gibson Les Paul Deluxe Gold Top quite a lot for the jazz albums I was doing at the time.

Gibson P-90

This is a perfect example of a classic high-output single-coil pickup. I tell you, these pickups are like a '59 Chevy truck. There is nothing that needs to be done—perfect as is. I've played a lot of P-90s, but the Gibson ones are the real deal! I played a Les Paul Studio '60s Tribute that came equipped with a pair of Gibson P-90 single-coil pickups, and they were built like a brick house. These stock pickups were hotter than some of the humbuckers I've played. What killer tone, through a Mesa Boogie, but the point is that this cheap guitar, as far as Les Pauls go, really kicked booty with these P-90s. The only downside is the single coil pick-ups, so when recording you are going to get hum and buzz that will have to be adjusted during the session—but it'll be well worth it. There are other manufacturers who make humless P-90s, but you lose all of the tone, so it is a tradeoff.

DiMarzio Super Distortion

The early days of companies that offered after-market replacement pickups for guitars were non-existent, and you were stuck with what came with the guitar stock. In the '70s, that all changed with companies like Seymour Duncan and DiMarzio. The Super Distortion was one of the first pickups offered that was a real hybrid PAF that could be easily replaced in guitars. It was a real steroids pickup with heavy sustain and overdrive monster that was an instant favorite among hard-rock shredders in the '80s. Ace Frehley of KISS comes to mind, as well as the maestro himself, Steve Vai. Those low-string pinch harmonics that you heard in the '80s were all attributed to this pickup. I believe Van Halen had a lot to do with the sound of those days, and since you couldn't buy his pickups, this was a good substitute.

DiMarzio Virtual P-90

These are high-output P-90 pickups, with a nice fullness to them without the muddiness. The two coils being tuned to different frequency ranges and output voltages removes that 60-cycle hum that I spoke about early. So you can adjust tone and balance by pole-piece heights, which is a great idea. The higher the pole piece, the louder the signal; based on the string, you can adjust the volume individually. It's perfect for those classic blues tones and clean jazz tones.

I had this in another Les Paul Deluxe and ran it through an Orange amp with awesome results. There was a nice boost in midfrequencies, while the low end had a real punch to it, plus the top strings did not sound brittle.

Using the right amp with the pickup choice is always an important factor. I also used the Mesa Boogie Mark II; the overdrive was very full with these pickups, working perfect on jazz chords.

Analog Tape and Why?

Yes, you read it right—analog tape! Everything can't be in this invisible Internet DAW world. Don't get me wrong; I like browsing on eBay and Craigslist as much as the next guy, but when recording, I want to be a bit more particular. Besides being a true analog aficionado, I have Pro Tools, Logic, Digital Performer, Reason, Live, et cetera, but with the best so-called converters, I still don't think sounds are as warm and natural as on tape. If they were, you wouldn't have people constantly trying to get tape emulators, or inventions like the CLASP, recording off of the tape heads on your analog tape machine and into your DAW and the older RADAR.

There is a market out there to get an analog sound on your digital computer—two entirely different formats, which is strange if you ask me. Why don't you just record on analog if you want an analog sound?

On certain projects I know there will be a lot changes, especially on the TV or film projects I compose. Sure, I'm going to use Pro Tools then. I simply need to get along in the world we live in. But on album projects, that's a whole different story. This is like trying to use a mouse to do an oil painting on a computer running an oil paint emulator program—and expecting it to hang in the Metropolitan Museum next to Edgar Degas's "The Dance Class" and Rembrandt's "Aristotle with a Bust of Homer." Come on; give me a break! Let's take some pride and time in recording to get it the best it can be.

But I will tell you that a little goes a long way. For instance, go out and buy an old two-track mixdown machine, such as an Otari MTR-10 or an Ampex ATR-102, and buy a new alignment tape to align and mix out of your DAW to tape—you'll find a world of difference just in that step. I do this all the time for the various TV shows for which I compose. Just recently, I mixed down some cues for *Extra* and *TMZ*, to my Otari 1/4-inch two-track. It really fattens the digital domain sound and warms up the entire mix.

If you search hard enough, you can get these old machines for a steal; in fact, I bought the Otari for $350 at an old music store in the East Village of NYC. What is the point of buying an analog tape machine emulator plug-in for basically the same price? It's just an imitation—you might as well buy the real thing. Plus, you can buy new old stock tape on eBay and other online stores. In fact, the two manufacturers left in the world that still make tape are ATR Magnetics (www.atrtape.com) and RMG International (www.rmgi.eu). Join the fun, man—there ain't nothing like tape!

Tricks, Tips, and Advice to Get That Mix Right

Here is a summary of some tips and tricks from pros that may help you through the recording process.

Shel Talmy

"I used to bring up two channels of the same thing, one that was heavily limited, and keep it under the other track. This helped push up apparent level so in the final product it would always sound louder."

"I spent a lot of time on baffling the instruments because I thought isolation was one of the major problems that was going on in the industry."

"For acoustic guitars I used two U 87s, one pointing at the sound hole and the other at the fretboard, and then I would combine them. I also would use an 1176 with a little EQ, which gave more apparent level to the acoustic."

Barry Conley

"I use a 57 on axis to the speaker and use a 421 off axis. The 57 is the bright, and the 421 is the fatness—and, of course, there is going to be some phase cancellation, but it works for guitars. So I used that, and it just seems to work great."

"The original 409 with the gold front and a ribbon mic M 160 work really well together. I like to keep both the ribbon and the 409 on the same axis to amp, so I don't get the phase cancellation. That way both mics are the same distance from the diaphragm of the speaker."

"B.B. came in with a reissue twin, and I miked it with a 57 and a 421 and put it in a couple of 1073s. It always seems to work for me. I stay away from 87s on guitar."

Marc DeSisto

"My go-to microphones are Shure 57 and a 414 together. I face them at a 45-degree angle with the two capsules touching, facing the opposite sides of the cones. I usually have a pad on the 414 and get a sound, and then I add the 57 slowly. The trick is to get them both at the same level, so you have the guitarist give a G chord and I see where the peak is on the 57, say –7 dB. Okay, I'd set the 57 to that –7 mark, bring the same thing up on the 414, and get that to –7."

"Another combination for me is a 57 and Beyer M 160, which is an amazing microphone. They are the most underrated microphones ever. It's unbelievable, I did this track with Don Henley on the The End of the Innocence album called 'Heart of the Matter'—it's a Vox amp off of the floor, and you hear it, and it's so perfect."

"For guitars it is an API 312 or a Neve 1073 or 1081. API or Neve is what I would be looking for first. It's all about getting the ambience around the guitar correctly. I look around the room to see what kind of reflection is going to go back into the mic; if you are in a small room, you'll hear it. I may put the amp kitty-corner so as to get less reflection."

Andy Wright

"*Jeff's technician arrived for the preproduction with a Marshall JCM800 top, a 4 × 12 cabinet, a Fender Stratocaster, and a Cry Baby wah pedal. We stuck the amp in the vocal booth of my programming room and stuck an SM57 in front of the cabinet about two inches from the middle. The mic was jammed at the other end into an Urei 1176 and from there straight into a Digidesign 888.*"

"*I created the filter up section on 'Earthquake' by utilizing the input on the Waldorf Pulse synth. I also had a selection of Lovetone pedals (the Meatball, Big Cheese, and Brown Sauce, and also, I think, the Ringstinger ring modulator), which I fed some sounds through.*"

Flemming Rasmussen

"*The first two albums, all mics went through my Trident A-range console. In those days we used the mic pres in the console. Very few people had external mic pres.*"

"*On all albums the main mics are Shure SM7 and Neumann U 87 close-miked, pointing to the center of one of the speaker cones. (Most guitars were recorded using two cabinets.) Then at an angle of 45 degrees from the corner of the cab and three to six feet away, I used AKG Gold Tube mics, one on each cabinet. As room mics I used Brüel and Kjaer (now Danish Audio Design) 4006 omnis, aproximately 10 to 15 feet away.*"

"*The source is always the most important. You can't save a bad guitar sound with EQs and compressors.*"

Guy Charbonneau

"*Lots of times I use a Shure 57 or a Royer, but with a live show you are sort of tied to the venue. Sometimes we have great sound because the sound becomes a part of the performance.*"

"*We have three systems to choose from when we go on the road for mobile recording: Le Mobile, the full truck recording system with the Neve 8058 (48 automated faders) recording console; Le Fly-Pak with 64 tracks of Pro Tools HD; and Le Box, a compact and affordable digital recording solution on the Nuendo system or on Pro Tools 9.*"

"*I try to mix it and do a full balance, with a sort of vibe of the mix. Then we bring in someone with fresh ears to listen, and we tweak the solos and other parts. It's nice to have someone in with a new perspective.*"

Chip Verspyck

"*I think the essential difference between analog tape and computer recording is the working environment. Tape limits your choices and makes you commit, forces you to work harder and perform better.*"

"Your best-sounding recording gear is only going to sound as good as the performance and space you're capturing, so you should first put your dollars and efforts into making it so the acoustics of your room are good enough. You also need good accurate monitors."

"Guitar amp distortion is an extreme form of compression. When your amp starts to distort, the crests of your sound waves are getting cut off as you run out of headroom, which limits volume. Your sound will only get so loud. Add a tube rectifier, and you get even more compression as the power supply voltage sags down and limits volume the harder you play."

Billy Sheehan

"I'm all digital. We use Logic, Pro Tools, Digital Performer, and Cubase too, but I've been using Logic mostly. I use MOTU interfaces and a Yamaha 02R96 to route everything where it needs to go."

Steve Vai

"I always keep a pair of C14s and a pair of 414s spread apart in the corners of the room. This is mixed into the sound at various levels depending on the desired effect. It's important to me to try and create a space for each guitar; the song should tell you what to do."

Will Ray

"The 1993 G&L ASAT Special and 1996 Fender Will Ray Mojo-Tele into a Carl Martin compressor, then into a Boss BCB- 3 pedal board, which has an Ibanez TS-5 Tube Screamer. I also took the recorded POD signal and played it into a miked Rivera M100 combo amp to beef things up. At mix time I used a little of each."

Andy Timmons

"I used all SM57s for recording the guitar. We recorded all the basic tracks onto two-inch analog tape in an old Neve room just south of Dallas, and then we bounced to Pro Tools, then to Logic to record the guitar tracks, bouncing everything back to Pro Tools for the final mix."

Eric Johnson

"I have a couple of different Marshalls with a little different circuitry. Some are more Hendrix rhythm, big Fender-sounding, and not as grainy with bigger, thicker rhythm tones and overdrive. Then I have some that are more Super Lead JMP that have a lot of gain within the amp."

Tommy Emmanuel

"I used a Neumann KM 184 pointing down the neck of the guitar toward the sound hole. Right in front of me, I used a handmade mic similar to an old Telefunken 251 and centered it to the sound hole about eight inches in front of me."

Howard Hart

"Believe it or not, I still love a Shure 57 for guitars. Close-miking is cool for certain things, but I actually like to back off the amp a bit—maybe four or five feet back and up a bit."

Steve Morse

"I'm attached to my old board, which is still wired to my old Studer 24-track, so everything went through the board on its way to being recorded by the computer. The old Urei compressors still work and are used on all vocals and clean guitars."

Robin Trower

"I used 2 Cornell Plexi 18/20 amps—these are the 20-watt 1 × 12 combos. I would split them from my pedals, running one clean and one more overdriven."

Zakk Wylde

"I'll bring the Les Paul and the Rock Replica Randy Rhoads Polka Dot V guitar made by GMW Guitar Works that I like to use on solos. I will also use a 12-string and 6-string acoustic—I bring the whole arsenal."

Larry Carlton

"My '69 that I've played for years is subtly different in many ways from a stock 335. I just got lucky in 1969 when I picked my 335 at a music store; out of the three or four they had, I picked the best-sounding one. And sure enough, that sucker is warm, not dark. Sings like an angel, but not bright."

Ted Nugent

"Ah yes, the sweet smoky BBQ grease drip of the mighty Gibson Byrdland in the hands of a pure, primal-scream aboriginal dogman fresh from a steaming gut pile campfire somewhere way back in the spirit wild hinterland that we all love so dearly. Such romance!"

Gary Hoey

"I used a few pedals. My signature pedal, Skull Crusher by HomeBrew Electronics, has a gain boost with a fat compression and not a lot of crunch. I also used the Power Screamer by HBE, the Rocktron Metal Planet, and the Austin Distortion."

Geoff Gray

"Generally in the smaller rooms I go to a 57 or 58 off-axis and close to the grill. We use the big room often for overdubs, and that is perfect for the Royer 122s and back about 18 inches.

Chuck Loeb

"I always go back to my CAE preamp for the 'super clean' sound, and I have a new pre called Tube Top from Japan. I love the Roland GT-10 and Line 6 M13 for quick-and-easy setups at live gigs and festivals."

Chris Poland

"Use your ears and don't follow the 'rules' of recording. If you like how you are sounding, then record it, so you don't lose what is happening at that moment."

Hal Lindes

"Shake it up, get inspired, be adventurous—and most importantly, enjoy yourself. After all, it's only rock-n-roll!"

5 Microphones for Tones

In the pro audio world, with so many choices for recording instruments, microphones have become a paramount ingredient. Mics are the true translation of guitar tones to recording and should be as accurate as possible. Every guitarist wants to record the sound he hears in the room through the amp. The question becomes, "How?"

Like everything else in life, there are thousands of interpretations of why certain mics are better than others. I always like speaking to guitarists about how they get their tone and capture it on a recording.

Beyerdynamic M 160

The M 160 has to be one of my favorite guitar microphones (see Figure 5.1). It's a very simple design but extremely effective for recording guitars. The mic's characteristics are very clean sounding, with a nice punch to the upper-mid frequencies. Because it is a ribbon mic, it really captures the nuances of the guitar and amp.

It's hard to believe that the company states that the manufacturing process for the M 160 has remained fundamentally unchanged since the model was introduced in 1957. Ironically, it was originally developed as an alternative to the then-expensive condenser microphone. Now a days, it seems that ribbon microphones have made a huge comeback and have become well known for their accurate reproduction.

Royer R-101

The R-101 is a mono, passive ribbon microphone utilizing an offset-ribbon transducer and a 2.5-micron ribbon element (see Figure 5.2). These microphones are considered to be the new breed of ribbon microphones, designed particularly for electric guitar cabinets. They feature an advanced multilayered windscreen for protection from air blasts and plosives, an internally shock-mounted ribbon transducer system, and a reduced proximity effect for closer miking with less bass buildup, especially on large amp cabinets.

Just place this mic as close as you like to the speaker and play loud and proud. I've used it on 4 × 12 cabinets, and they sound very good, keeping the full body of the sound without being too

Image by Ricky Restiano.

Figure 5.1   Beyerdynamic M 160.

muddy. In combination with a Shure SM57 and a Sennheiser MD 421, you get a great combination of textures that can be blended in the final mix (see Figure 5.3). The R-101 retains the midrange frequencies very well, creating a smooth response. They are also very good on acoustic guitar. The ribbon element responds very well, capturing the natural wood sound and the metallic ringing of the strings.

sE Voodoo VR1

The sE Voodoo has to be one of the nicest ribbon microphones on the market today (see Figure 5.4). It performs across 20 Hz to 20 kHz, which is a direct result of the Rupert Neve collaboration with sE. This was made possible by using state-of-the-art transformers and a Rupert-designed circuit board to reveal HF (high frequency), which is usually absent.

What you get is a whole new sound different from any other ribbon on the market. This enables the Voodoo to extend performance, which had not previously been possible, except in condenser

Figure 5.2   Royer R-101.

Figure 5.3   Shure SM57, Royer R-101, and Sennheiser MD 421.

Image by Ricky Restiano.

Figure 5.4 sE Voodoo VR1.

microphones. I found it to have a fuller frequency range, and on a guitar cabinet to really capture those mid- and high-range frequencies. The Voodoo really records the detail of the guitar, enabling you to hear the fingers on the fretboard. This makes the job of placing the guitar in the mix so much easier—the guitar stands out but has nice seating in the final mix. It's perfect on acoustic guitars, too, by placing the microphone by the 12th fret pointing down toward the sound hole. It's great because there is no proximity effect, capturing the pristineness of the instrument.

sE RT1 Ribbon Tube

The RT1 is probably one of the best ribbon tube microphones. Unlike other ribbon mics, in which you have to really push the gain on the preamp to get the output up, the RT1 has its own power supply. Thus, it has plenty of gain to print on tape directly!

I find it to be a very smooth microphone with the warmth of the tube, making it a real vintage piece right out of the box. It's absolutely fantastic on electric guitar cabinets, in any shape or size. Many times I record two amps at a time through the Framptone Amp Switcher, using the RT1 on a Soldano Reverb-O-Sonic 4 × 10 (see Figure 5.5) and a Sennheiser 421 on a Fender Showman 4 × 12 cabinet (see Figure 5.6). For a clean-sounding strat tone, this microphone is the one. It adds a nice silky sheen to the recording without coloring the tone of the source. It's a real tone-capturing microphone for guitars!

Figure 5.5 sE RT1 Ribbon Tube.

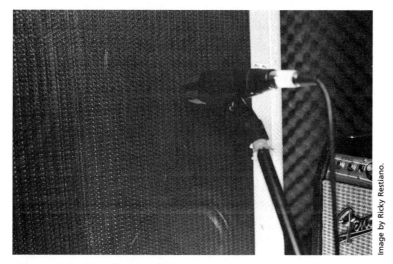

Figure 5.6 Sennheiser 421.

Sennheiser e 609

The Sennheiser e 609 is able to withstand high SPLs (*sound pressure levels*) without distorting—now that's what I want to hear (see Figure 5.7)! The 609 Silver's flat-profile capsule facilitates extremely close miking of guitar cabinets. This is a result from the supercardioid design that

Image by Ricky Restiano.

Figure 5.7   Sennheiser e 609.

improves isolation especially in live sound and studio recording. This all creates a wider frequency response and an increased output, improving the overall performance.

Though the 609 does not have the articulation and dynamics that the new ribbon microphones have, it still records a fat sound from cabinets. The beauty of it is its simplicity and ease of use. This is a perfect microphone when cutting tracks with a live band because of the supercardioid pickup pattern that provides isolation from other surrounding instrument signals. The 609 is great to use in conjunction with a ribbon mic such as the M 160 when miking an open-back amp, such as the Fender Super Reverb (see Figure 5.8).

AKG C 414

The 414 is the mother ship of microphones. For more than 60 years, engineers and producers have used the 414 for almost every imaginable application. It has become the reference microphone for almost all comparative microphone tests and is one of the most used condenser microphones in the world. It boosts a gold-sputtered 1-inch dual-diaphragm; a selectable cardioid of hypercardioid, omnidirectional, or figure-eight polar patterns; a two-stage preattenuation pad and bass cut filter; and a high sound pressure level capability of up to 160 dB SPL.

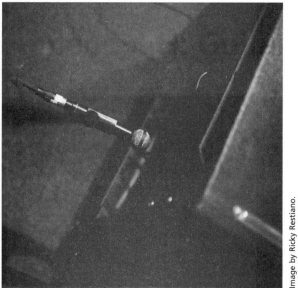

Figure 5.8   Beyerdynamic M 160.

This is the real deal in studio microphones. It shines on so many instruments, from horns to acoustic guitar to overhead drum mics. I love it on acoustic guitar. With a little experimenting and moving it around in front of the guitar, you can get a really natural recording. I usually place it between the 12th fret and the sound hole of the guitar pointing down toward the bridge (see Figure 5.9). As we saw

Figure 5.9   AKG C 414.

earlier, engineer-producers Barry Conley and Marc DeSisto have their own techniques to record guitar cabinets with the 414. It also makes a terrific room mic on guitar cabinets (see Figure 5.10).

Figure 5.10   AKG 414 room mic.

Shure SM57

What can be said about the Shure SM57 (see Figure 5.11) that hasn't already been said? This is the microphone you're sure to find in every live venue, recording studio, and school band room around the world. It is the true workhorse of microphones!

The SM57 is cheap and effective, and it loves electric guitar cabinets. Every guitarist should have at least one of these glued to his amp for backup. As you've seen throughout the book, the 57 is still the most popular mic used by both artists and engineers. An old favorite microphone combination is placing the 57 about an inch away from the center of the speaker cone and then combining it with a Sennheiser MD 421 on the right side of the 57 at a 45-degree angle and keeping it the same distance from the speaker (see Figure 5.12). You record each mic on its own track and blend according to taste. You'll get a nice beefy tone. The 421 will provide the body of the tone, and the 57 will record the higher frequencies of the guitar, making it a perfect match.

Sennheiser MD 421

Put simply, the 421 is an SM57 on steroids. It's probably one of the most diverse mics ever made. It is most commonly used for miking toms, but it has so much more potential. In fact, the

Image by Ricky Restiano.

Figure 5.11   Shure SM57.

421 shines in broadcasting applications, such as radio announcing, featuring the five-position bass control, which enhances its all-around qualities.

The wonderful advantage of the 421 is that it handles very high SPLs. It was born to be a rock guitar mic. Being a large-diaphragm dynamic microphone that came out originally in the early '60s, the 421 has been on almost every classic rock recording in some way or another.

Neumann TLM 49

The TLM 49 is a solid-state cardioid microphone with warm characteristics. I've used these mics on everything from guitar cabinets to sax, vocals, and even piano (in a stereo pair). I usually use it in conjunction with another mic when recording guitar cabinets. For instance, I'll near-mike a Marshall cabinet with an M 160 and place the TLM 49 about five feet back. You get a nice clear image with the M 160 and a thicker cabinet sound of the room with the TLM 49. I blend these two signals together during the mix, placing the M 160 signal a bit higher, while fading just enough of the TLM 149 to create a thicker depth of the guitar. Because the TLM 49 is a large-diaphragm microphone, I feel it captures a fuller, warmer sound of the guitar cabinets, creating a realistic recording of the sound you hear in the room.

Image by Ricky Restiano.

Figure 5.12   Shure SM57 and Sennheiser MD 421.

Image by Ricky Restiano.

Figure 5.13   Sennheiser MD 421.

Image by Ricky Restiano.

Figure 5.14   Neumann TLM 49.

AKG D 112

I use this method on many bass recordings through the Radial J48 Direct Box as a buffer to split the signal. I plug the amp into the Radials Thru jack and plug the bass into the input. I'll then take the XLR signal directly to one track and print the miked signal.

This gives me the flexibility to blend the direct signal a little lower during mixdown, which I find adds full body to the bass sound. For solo bass tracks, it adds a wonderful depth of sound to the bass and gives the engineer flexibility when mixing. You can also do a nice stereo pan with the two signals, enabling you to EQ and affect the signals differently.

Electro-Voice RE20

Now the RE20 Variable-D dynamic cardioid microphone is truly an industry standard, but not as a guitar microphone. Instead it is used in the broadcast industry as an announcer mic. It features the EVs Variable-D design along with the heavy-duty internal P-pop filter, which reduces proximity effect. It's made like a brick house with an internal element shock-mount that reduces

Image by Ricky Restiano.

Figure 5.15   AKG D 112.

vibration noise. It even has a bass roll off-switch to use if things get too boomy from the amp. But this is the designated bass mic for me.

I place it directly in front of the 15-inch bass cabinet speaker, a little offset from the voice coil (see Figure 5.16). It adds no colorization to the tone and captures the bass quite accurately. The RE20 has always been popularly used to mike a kick drum and floor toms, again resulting in an excellent sound.

AKG C 1000 S

Another extremely versatile microphone is the AKG C 1000 S, ideally suited for all kinds of recording and live sound reinforcement. A standard 9-volt battery or the phantom power from a mixer can power the mic. What's very useful is that the polar pattern can quickly be switched from cardioid to hypercardioid simply by attaching the provided PPC 1000 Polar Pattern Converter to the microphone capsule. There is also an adapter, called the PB 1000 Presence Boost, which adds 3 to 5 dB of high-end enhancement, improving clarity of speech and adding definition to instrument sounds.

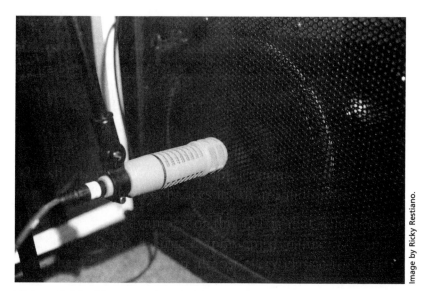

Image by Ricky Restiano.

Figure 5.16 Electro-Voice RE20.

I really like this on acoustic guitars, placing it between the sound whole and the 15th fret, angled a bit toward the body (see Figure 5.17). Like many other microphones we've discussed, the 1000 S is great when used in conjunction with another mic—for instance, when adding a 414 over the right shoulder of the player to capture the room sound of the guitar, blending it in with the 1000 S.

Image by Ricky Restiano.

Figure 5.17 AKG C 1000 S.

LR Baggs Microphone System

Leo Kottke used the first LR Baggs product, the LB6 Series Pickup. The octave Acoustic Guitar Pickup System combines an all-discrete, Class A FET preamp built on a stereo strapjack. It is assisted by an internal mic that is connected underneath the guitar top. The preamp also features a second octave input, so you can easily run a second pickup to complement the LR Baggs. It is an incredible system and completely preserves the integrity of the acoustic tone. I usually plug directly into the Universal Audio 610 mic preamp and record. With its various contour controls, plus the EQ control on the 610, the Baggs makes getting the right tone a breeze. Combine this system with any of the mics already discussed, such as the 414 or the TLM 49, and you'll get an extremely full sound. Also, try panning the Baggs to the right and the TLM 49 to the left and placing the 414 straight up at 12 o'clock in the mix.

Image by Ricky Restiano.

Figure 5.18   LR Baggs.

Conclusion

Most of these mics aren't terribly expensive. Prices can range anywhere from $200 to $1,500, which is worth it when it comes to achieving great guitar tones in your recordings. To be quite honest, I find that many artists tend to fall back on the less expensive, reliable SM57, especially after trying other mics.

I always find that by experimenting you get the best results; hence, multi-miking is a great avenue for covering your bases. Often you may find you like the sound of two mics combined, but when soloed, the sound may not be as good—or vice versa.

Also, keep in mind how the guitar tracks sit in the song. Spending a lot of time getting a huge, overdriven guitar tone for a reggae song may not be the right direction to go. All of us have been in that boat at some time or another—working diligently on recording the best tone for the guitar part, only to realize that the guitar sounds great but does not fit the track at all. However, these mics will give you the tools for getting your guitar tones recorded. So when approaching all of these mics, think in terms as a producer as well as a guitarist.

Appendix A: iTunes Best Guitar Songs

1. Artist: Steve Morse
   Track: "Cruise Missile"
   Album: *The Introduction*

2. Artist: Jimmy Page
   Track: "Emerald Eyes"
   Album: *Outrider*

3. Artist: John Paul Jones
   Track: "Zooma"
   Album: *Zooma*

4. Artist: Jeff Beck
   Track: "Blow By Blow"
   Album: *You Know What I Mean*

5. Artist: Jeff Beck
   Track: "Freeway Jam"
   Album: *Jeff Beck with the Jan Hammer Group Live*

6. Artist: Jeff Beck
   Track: "Goodbye Pork Pie Hat"
   Album: *Wired*

7. Artist: Jeff Beck
   Track: "Earthquake"
   Album: *You Had It Coming*

8. Artist: Tony Williams (featuring Alan Holdsworth)
   Track: "Proto-Cosmos"
   Album: *Lifetime: The Collection CD*

9. Artist: Billy Cobham (featuring John Scofield)
    Track: "East Bay"
    Album: *Life & Times*

10. Artist: Billy Cobham (featuring Tommy Bolin)
    Track: "Red Baron"
    Album: *Spectrum*

11. Artist: Ohm (featuring Chris Poland)
    Track: "Peanut Buddha"
    Album: *Ohm*

12. Artist: John Mayall & The Blues Breakers
    Track: "Steppin' Out"
    Album: *Blues Breakers with Eric Clapton*

13. Artist: George Benson
    Track: "Little Train (From Bachianas Brasileiras #2)"
    Album: *White Rabbit*

14. Artist: John Scofield
    Track: "Blue Matter"
    Album: *Blue Matter*

15. Artist: Steve Vai
    Track: "The Attitude Song"
    Album: *Flex-Able*

16. Artist: Steve Vai
    Track: "Call It Sleep"
    Album: *Flex-Able*

17. Artist: Steve Vai
    Track: "The Animal"
    Album: *Passion and Warfare*

18. Artist: Joe Satriani
    Track: "Ice 9"
    Album: *Surfing with the Alien*

19. Artist: Joe Satriani
    Track: "Back to Shalla-Bal"
    Album: *Flying in a Blue Dream*

20. Artist: Joe Satriani
    Track: "Devil's Slide"
    Album: *Engines of Creation*

21. Artist: Zakk Wylde
    Track: "Sold My Soul"
    Album: *Book of Shadows*

22. Artist: Black Label Society featuring Zakk Wylde
    Track: "Faith Is Blind"
    Album: *Shot to Hell*

23. Artist: Larry Carlton
    Track: "Double Cross"
    Album: *Fire Wire*

24. Artist: Larry Carlton
    Track: "Big Trouble"
    Album: *Fire Wire*

25. Artist: Cream
    Track: "Sleepy Time Time"
    Album: *Live Cream*

26. Artist: Johnny Winter
    Track: "Rock Me Baby"
    Album: *Still Alive and Well*

27. Artist: Johnny Winter
    Track: "Rock & Roll"
    Album: *Still Alive and Well*

28. Artist: Ace Frehley
    Track: "Genghis Khan"
    Album: *Anomaly*

29. Artist: Blue Murder
     Track: "Billy"
     Album: *Blue Murder*

30. Artist: Stevie Ray Vaughan and Double Trouble
     Track: "Scuttle Buttin'"
     Album: *Couldn't Stand the Weather*

31. Artist: Stevie Ray Vaughan and Double Trouble
     Track: "Couldn't Stand the Weather"
     Album: *Couldn't Stand the Weather*

32. Artist: Jimi Hendrix
     Track: "Spanish Castle Magic"
     Album: *Live at Woodstock*

33. Artist: Jimi Hendrix
     Track: "Voodoo Child"
     Album: *Live at Woodstock*

34. Artist: Albert King with Stevie Ray Vaughan
     Track: "Ask Me No Questions"
     Album: *In Session*

35. Artist: Pat Travers
     Track: "Snortin' Whiskey"
     Album: *Crash and Burn*

36. Artist: Pat Travers
     Track: "Born Under a Bad Sign"
     Album: *Crash and Burn*

37. Artist: Eric Johnson
     Track: "Columbia"
     Album: *Bloom*

38. Artist: Eric Johnson
     Track: "Summer Jam"
     Album: *Bloom*

39. Artist: Eric Johnson
     Track: "Camel's Night Out"
     Album: *Venus Isle*

40. Artist: Eric Johnson
     Track: "Cliffs of Dover"
     Album: *Live from Austin TX*

41. Artist: Santana
     Track: "Soweto (Africa Libre)"
     Album: *Spirits Dancing in the Flesh*

42. Artist: Santana
     Track: "Peace on Earth...Mother Earth...Third Stone from the Sun"
     Album: *Spirits Dancing in the Flesh*

43. Artist: Santana
     Track: "Bailando/Aquatic Park"
     Album: *Blues for Salvador*

44. Artist: Billy Sheehan
     Track: "Suspense Is Killing Me"
     Album: *Cosmic Troubadour*

45. Artist: Niacin
     Track: "Mean Streets"
     Album: *Deep*

46. Artist: Gary Moore
     Track: "I Can't Quit You Baby"
     Album: *Power of the Blues*

47. Artist: Gary Moore
     Track: "Only Fool in Town"
     Album: *After Hours*

48. Artist: The Mahavishnu Orchestra with John McLaughlin
     Track: "Vital Transformation"
     Album: *The Inner Mounting Flame*

49. Artist: Revocation
     Track: "Alliance in Tyranny"
     Album: *Empire of the Obscene*

50. Artist: Meshuggah
     Track: "Dancers to a Discordant System"
     Album: *ObZen*

51. Artist: Michael Hedges
     Track: "Ragamuffin"
     Album: *Aerial Boundaries*

Appendix B: YouTube Best Guitar Videos

1. Artist: Frank Zappa
   Track: "Muffin Man"
   Link: www.youtube.com/user/ashtrayheart23

2. Artist: Billy Sheehan
   Track: "Billy Sheehan Bass Solo"
   Link: www.youtube.com/user/joeroman81

3. Artist: John Paul Jones
   Track: "Tidal"
   Link: www.youtube.com/user/holtinator

4. Artist: Steve Vai
   Track: "I Know You're Here"
   Link: www.youtube.com/user/SteveVaiHimself

5. Artist: Jimmy Page
   Track: "Kashmir Chords"
   Link: www.youtube.com/user/djlightbolt

6. Artist: Ozzy featuring Randy Rhoads
   Track: "After Hours (Live)"
   Link: www.youtube.com/user/electricangel23666

7. Artist: Les Paul
   Track: "Chasing Sound"
   Link: www.youtube.com/user/gianniparadiso

8. Artist: Alan Holdsworth
    Track: "Looking Glass"
    Link: www.youtube.com/user/eugbreh

9. Artist: Robin Trower
    Track: "Too Rolling Stoned (Live)"
    Link: www.youtube.com/user/Davebritbrat

Appendix C: Performance Rights Organizations

Definition: PROs provide royalty collection between copyright holders and parties who wish to use copyrighted works *publicly*, especially the performing of music on radio and television programs. In the USA, the companies SESAC, ASCAP, and BMI collect license fees on behalf of songwriters, composers, and music publishers and distribute them as royalties to those members whose works have been performed.

1. PRO: SESAC
   Country: USA
   Link: www.sesac.com

2. PRO: ASCAP
   Country: USA
   Link: www.ascap.com

3. PRO: BMI
   Country: USA
   Link: www.bmi.com

4. PRO: PRS for Music
   Country: United Kingdom
   Link: www.prsformusic.com

5. PRO: SADAIC
   Country: Argentina
   Link: www.sadaic.org.ar

6. PRO: APRA/AMCOS
   Country: Australia
   Link: www.apra-amcos.com.au

7. PRO: AKM
   Country: Austria
   Link: www.akm.at

8. PRO: SABAM
   Country: Belgium
   Link: www.sabam.be

9. PRO: UBE, ECAD
   Country: Brazil
   Link: www.ubc.org.br, www.ecad.org.br

10. PRO: MUSICAUTOR
    Country: Bulgaria
    Link: www.musicautor.org

11. PRO: SOCAN
    Country: Canada
    Link: www.socan.ca

12. PRO: SCD
    Country: Chile
    Link: www.scd.cl

13. PRO: SAYCO
    Country: Colombia
    Link: www.sayco.org

14. PRO: HDS
    Country: Croatia
    Link: www.hds.hr

15. PRO: OSA
    Country: Czech Republic
    Link: www.osa.cz

16. PRO: KODA
    Country: Denmark
    Link: www.koda.dk

17. PRO: EAU
     Country: Estonia
     Link: www.eau.org

18. PRO: TEOSTO
     Country: Finland
     Link: www.teosto.fi

19. PRO: SACEM
     Country: France
     Link: www.sacem.fr

20. PRO: GEMA
     Country: Germany
     Link: www.gema.de

21. PRO: AEPI
     Country: Greece
     Link: www.aepi.gr

22. PRO: CASH
     Country: Hong Kong
     Link: www.cash.org.hk

23. PRO: ARTISJUS
     Country: Hungary
     Link: www.artisjus.hu

24. PRO: LISTIR
     Country: Iceland
     Link: www.stef.is

25. PRO: IPRS
     Country: India
     Link: www.iprs.org

26. PRO: IMRO
     Country: Ireland
     Link: www.imro.ie

27. PRO: ACUM
     Country: Israel
     Link: www.acum.org.il

28. PRO: SIAE
     Country: Italy
     Link: www.siae.it

29. PRO: JASRAC
     Country: Japan
     Link: www.jasrac.or.jp

30. PRO: LATGA
     Country: Lithuania
     Link: www.latga.lt

31. PRO: MACP
     Country: Malaysia
     Link: www.macp.com.my

32. PRO: SACM
     Country: Mexico
     Link: www.sacm.org.mx

33. PRO: BUMA
     Country: Netherlands
     Link: www.buma.nl

34. PRO: APRA/AMCOS
     Country: New Zealand
     Link: www.apra-amcos.com.au

35. PRO: TONO
     Country: Norway
     Link: www.tono.no

36. PRO: ZAIKS
     Country: Poland
     Link: www.zaiks.org.pl

37. PRO: SPA
    Country: Portugal
    Link: www.spautores.pt

38. PRO: RAO
    Country: Russia
    Link: www.rao.ru/orao

39. PRO: COMPASS
    Country: Singapore
    Link: www.compass.org.sg

40. PRO: SAMRO
    Country: South Africa
    Link: www.samro.org.za

41. PRO: SGAE
    Country: Spain
    Link: www.sgae.es

42. PRO: STIM
    Country: Sweden
    Link: www.stim.se

43. PRO: SUISA
    Country: Switzerland
    Link: www.suisa.ch

44. PRO: COTT
    Country: Trinidad and Tobago
    Link: www.cott.org.tt

45. PRO: MESAM
    Country: Turkey
    Link: www.mesam.org.tr

46. PRO: AGADU
    Country: Uruguay
    Link: www.agadu.com

Appendix D: Web References

1. Les Paul Online
   www.lespaulonline.com

2. Ultimate Guitar
   www.ultimate-guitar.com

3. Truth in Shredding
   www.truthinshredding.com

4. Audio Engineering Society
   www.aes.org

5. GC Pro
   www.gcpro.com

6. Manhatpro
   www.manhatpro.com/site

7. Acoustical Solutions
   www.acousticalsolutions.com

8. The National Academy of Television Arts & Sciences
   www.emmyonline.org

9. NARAS
   www.grammy.com

10. Cengage Learning
    www.cengage.com/us

11. Institute of Audio Research
     www.audioschool.com

12. The School of Audio Engineering (SAE)
     us.sae.edu

13. Hal Leonard
     www.halleonard.com

14. JRF Magnetics
     www.jrfmagnetics.com

15. Recording Consoles of the 20th Century
     www.recordingconsoles.net

Appendix E: Trade Magazines

1. *Recording*
   www.recordingmag.com

2. *Pro Sound News*
   www.prosoundnetwork.com/index

3. *Mix*
   www.mixonline.com

4. *Guitar Player*
   www.guitarplayer.com

5. *Vintage Guitar*
   www.vintageguitar.com

6. *Guitar World*
   www.guitarworld.com

7. *The Hollywood Reporter*
   www.hollywoodreporter.com

8. *Electronic Musician*
   www.emusician.com

9. *SESAC*
   www.sesac.com/News/Magazine.aspx

10. *Tape Op*
    www.tapeop.com

Appendix F: Highly Recommended Readings

1. Title: *Microphones*
   Author: Martin Clifford
   Publisher: TAB Books Inc. (1986)

2. Title: *Introduction to Professional Recording Techniques*
   Author: Bruce Bartlett
   Publisher: Howard W. Sams & Company (1987)

3. Title: *Jim Marshall: The Father of Loud*
   Author: Rich Maloof
   Publisher: Backbeat Books (2003)

4. Title: *Studio Stories*
   Author: David Simons
   Publisher: Backbeat Books (2004)

5. Title: *Sound Studio Construction on a Budget*
   Author: F. Alton Everest
   Publisher: McGraw-Hill (1996)

6. Title: *The Tube Amp Book*, 4.1th edition
   Author: Aspen Pittman
   Publisher: Groove Tubes, LLC (2002)

7. Title: *Behind the Glass*
   Author: Howard Massey
   Publisher: Backbeat Books (2000)

8. Title: *50 Years of the Gibson Les Paul*
   Author: Tony Bacon
   Publisher: Backbeat Books (2002)

9. Title: *The Tube Amp Book*
    Author: Aspen Pittman
    Publisher: Backbeat Books (2003)

10. Title: *Fender Amps: The First Fifty Years*
    Author: John Teagle and John Sprung
    Publisher: Hal Leonard (1995)

11. Title: *Home Recording Studio: Build It Like the Pros*
    Author: Rod Gervais
    Publisher: Course Technology PTR (2006)

12. Title: *Classic Guitars*
    Author: Walter Carter
    Publisher: Metro Books (2008)

13. Title: *The Recording Engineer's Handbook*
    Author: Bobby Owsinski
    Publisher: Course Technology PTR (2009)

14. Title: *Jimmy Page: Magus Musician Man*
    Author: George Case
    Publisher: Hal Leonard (2009)

15. Title: *The Fender Book*
    Author: Tony Bacon and Paul Day
    Publisher: Miller Freeman Books (1999)

Appendix G: Guitar Manufacturers

1. Gibson Guitars
   www2.gibson.com

2. Fender
   www.fender.com

3. Eastwood Guitars
   www.eastwoodguitars.com

4. Rickenbacker
   www.rickenbacker.com

5. Ibanez
   www.ibanez.com

6. Guild
   www.guildguitars.com

7. WD Music Products
   www.wdmusic.com

8. Steward-Macdonald
   www.stewmac.com

9. Warmoth
   www.warmoth.com

10. ESP
    www.espguitars.com

Appendix H: Guitar Amp Manufacturers

1. Marshall
   www.marshallamps.com

2. Fender
   www.fender.com

3. Mesa Engineering
   www.mesaboogie.com

4. Orange
   www.orangeamps.com

5. Epiphone
   www.epiphone.com

6. Traynor
   www.traynoramps.com

7. Industrial Amps
   www.industrialamps.com

8. SUNN
   www.sunnamps.com

9. Blackstar Amplification
   www.blackstaramps.co.uk

10. HIWATT
    www.hiwatt.com/index2.html

Appendix I: Guitar Accessory Companies

1. Dunlop
   www.jimdunlop.com

2. Framptone
   www.framptone.com

3. Robert Keeley Electronics
   www.robertkeeley.com

4. Electro-Harmonix
   www.ehx.com

5. Snarling Dogs
   www.snarlingdogs.com

6. Eventide
   www.eventide.com

7. Boss
   www.bossus.com

8. DigiTech
   www.digitech.com

9. Seymour Duncan
   www.seymourduncan.com

10. Fulltone
    www.fulltone.com

Appendix J: Recording Manufacturers

1. Rupert Neve Designs
   www.rupertneve.com

2. Shure
   www.shure.com

3. Beyerdynamic
   www.beyerdynamic.com

4. ATR Magnetics
   www.atrtape.com

5. RMGI
   www.rmgi-usa.com

6. Toft Audio Designs
   www.toftaudio.com

7. JDK Audio
   www.jdkaudio.com

8. Manley
   www.manley.com

9. Tascam
   www.tascam.com

10. DBX
    www.dbxpro.com

Appendix K: Top 10 Guitar Websites

1. Ultimate Guitar
   www.ultimate-guitar.com

2. Truth In Shredding
   www.truthinshredding.com

3. Guitar Noize
   www.guitarnoize.com

4. Get Ready to Rock
   www.getreadytorock.com

5. Guitar Vibe
   www.guitarvibe.com

6. Guitar Player Zen
   www.guitarplayerzen.com

7. Atomic Guitarist
   www.atomicguitarist.com

8. GuitarGeek
   www.guitargeek.com

9. Strat-O-Blogster
   www.stratoblogster.com

10. Guitar Lifestyle
    www.guitarlifestyle.com

Index

Like the Book?

Let us know on Facebook or Twitter!

facebook.com/courseptr
twitter.com/courseptr

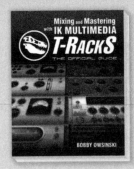
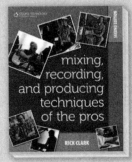